Wonky

Wonky

A Survival Guide for Following Jesus When You Hate the Church

Justin Bowers, PhD.

Foreword, J. Kevin Butcher

For Carrie, Malia, Pressley, Isabella, and Stephanie.
You live the wonkiness with me every, single day.

And for those who still believe in the fantastical dream of God's
Kingdom, even in spite of the Church.

CONTENTS

CONTENTS

Foreword

Renowned continental theologian Hans Urs von Balthasar once wrote, "Lovers are the ones who know most about God; the theologian must listen to them."[1] This is why I listen to Justin Bowers and why I'm convinced you need to read this book. Justin is a lover. He doesn't just believe in Jesus Christ, he loves him, as he is loved by him. And because of his deep love relationship with Jesus, Justin loves his family, his neighbors, the brothers and sisters he shepherds at New Community – and even his enemies. Not perfectly, of course, but make no mistake – the center of Justin's life is the deep love of Jesus Christ.

Not surprisingly, then, Justin's first book is about love, written especially to those of us who have not been loved well by the church. In fact, we've been deeply hurt. Because we've been judged. Gossiped about. Marginalized. Because her members have often co-opted Jesus for their political views, to excuse a lack of intentionality about fighting for justice, to justify both covert and overt racism, or to ignore hurtful behavior patterns (read "sin"). The truth is, Jesus calls us to radically give our lives away to others in deep relationship – in the church. But ironically, it's often the church that is the most self-absorbed, unloving, hurtful community on the planet.

As for a healing pathway forward – you'll find no cliches or easy answers here. In *Wonky*, Justin first acknowledges our "body of Christ pain" with love and compassion, authentically sharing – more than once – "I am so, truly, sorry" for the deep wounds that have driven his readers away from church. He candidly shares his own church hurt while also humbly, perhaps as proxy for other pastors, owning his culpability in hurting some he has pastored. Justin's obvious empathy for all who are bleeding out from church misbehavior gently invites us to position ourselves for the process of forgiveness and return. In other words, healing.

But Justin spends most of his time calling out specific areas of church dysfunction that create space for church wound – the undue pressure on pastors to be more than they can humanly be, pervasive relational division, the politicizing of Jesus, ignoring the gospel's call to racial justice, overlooking sin, the self-centered abuse of freedom – and more. Readers will find themselves nodding their heads at page after page of all-too-familiar mess and then they'll nod even more vigorously as Justin unpacks the instructive story of the early church (The Acts of the Apostles) and the wisdom of Paul (especially from I Corinthians) about the powerful, redemptive, healing force the church could be, *must be,* if our broken world is to have any hope of renewal.

Then, throughout *Wonky*, Justin appropriately provides hopeful hints about how to fight back against the powers of darkness disemboweling Christ's church. He calls them "church survival tips" and they vary from the obviously core "your relationship with Jesus must be stronger than your relationship with the church" to the very pragmatic "for any possibility of unity in the church, we must relinquish our right to be right." But even with Justin's pithy, wise, and helpful invitations to "do church differently", I found myself, by the end, looking for more.

Not surprisingly, Justin delivers. In the book's final pages, quoting Paul's words to the finger-pointing Corinthians, Justin calls us to first "examine ourselves" (I Corinthians 11:28), to stop focusing on the baggage of others in order to "deal with our own junk" as a precursor to slowly, courageously engaging Christ's church again. And the bottom line? In that process of re-engagement, of healing both ourselves and the church, Justin reminds us of the life-or-death priority of Paul's "most excellent way" – the powerful love of Jesus Christ. (I Corinthians 13) It was Christ's powerful love that defeated the powers of darkness at the cross, and his love in and through each of us is the only way the broken church of Jesus "can come to life again." In fact, Justin implies, unless we move beyond simply believing in Jesus to falling in love with him – we'll never come back to Christ's wounded church at all. The pain of church hurt will simply be...too much. Jesus' deep love, a love that "covers a multitude of sins", really is the only way.

Again, why does this really matter? Because the church of Jesus Christ – as wonky, wounded and wounding as it can often be – is still "the salt of the earth...the light of the world" (Matthew 5:13-16) There's no plan B for the hope and healing of all that is broken on planet earth, especially the broken hearts and lives of God's sons and daughters, which includes even those who don't yet know there is a God who loves them! They *must* see his healing love in us, in his church. Again, there is no other way.

Thus, the reason Justin writes with such passion. More importantly, despite being severely wounded himself, this is why Justin continues, day after day, to bring his wounded self to Jesus' wonky, broken church. This isn't the place for my own story, but trust me, my wife, three daughters and I have also been deeply hurt by the church. In 35 years of pastoral ministry, I, too, like Justin, have walked away in my mind dozens of times and have been tempted more than once to walk away – for good. But...we stay. Not because we're pious heroes – but because we know that if the broken world around us is to have any hope, we *must learn to love Christ's church over and over again. In and through the pain. All the way home.*

So, with compassion and empathy for *your* journey of church wound, I conclude my remarks, borrowing Justin's own concluding words: *"Don't ever give up."* If the church has broken your heart, *"may you find love for her again."* Because, my precious sister and brother, there really is...no other way.

[1] "Love Alone Is Credible", Hans urs Von Balthasar, Ignatius Press, 2004, p. 12.

J. KEVIN BUTCHER
Founder, Rooted Ministries (rootedministries.co)
Author, *Choose and Choose Again* and *Free*

Part One

Wonkified

"I've got a golden ticket!"

What a moment. Do you remember it?

The poor little urchin Charlie Bucket walking despondently down the street in London, having spent his last dollar on a candy bar in hopes of getting the remaining golden ticket that would grant him access to the mesmerizing world of the famous chocolatier Willy Wonka. In his sadness he glances down into a gutter to find a chocolate bar staring back at him. But not just any chocolate bar—no, a Wonka Bar! And as Charlie peels back the label to find the magic glint of the gold foil hidden within the wrapper, so his sadness peels away. In that moment, Charlie Bucket's world is forever changed. He will be granted access to Willy Wonka's chocolate factory.

Charlie and the Chocolate Factory. I love that movie. Not the Tim Burton remake with Johnny Depp and the weird squirrels. I love the Gene Wilder, musical extravaganza, creepy boat-ride included original. As a kid, I watched this film on VHS so many times I literally wore the tape out. . I loved how each of the rebellious, spoiled, gluttonous, or greedy young children faced the consequences of their own vices. And I loved the magic of what was behind the old factory doors of that mysterious chocolate factory. But I loved one scene more than any other.

It's early in the movie. In fact, it's right after Charlie finds his golden ticket. Each of the five winning children with their golden tickets are gathered outside the factory. They are surrounded by ravenous reporters and envious onlookers, security and admirers. They're standing, waiting, wondering if they'll truly meet the magical Willy Wonka of whom they've heard so many rumors.

Suddenly, the doors of the factory swing wide and there he is—Willy Wonka (played by the whimsical Gene Wilder), cloaked in that velvety purple jacket and distinctive top-hat. He looks so fragile, walking slowly, hobbling with a cane as he makes his way down the red carpet toward the children. Just when you think he can't move any slower, he stops in his tracks, cane standing on its own, and falls forward tumbling into a nimble roll and springing upward with nothing but a smile and arms held wide to welcome the children to the joyful pure-imagination world of his chocolate factory. I love that scene.

I remember watching it for the first time and recognizing how quickly my feelings changed about Mr. Willy Wonka. As he walks the carpet ever so slowly, I remember a bit of fear, some curiosity, and a good deal of confusion as to how this decrepit man could make such wonderfully known chocolate. But then, as he tumbled forward looking like he was about to make his final fall and suddenly rolled into a joyous host, my feelings shifted. Something changed. This journey had just become magical, and I was along for the ride.

When he was asked about this particular scene, Gene Wilder said: "When I make my first entrance, I'd like to come out of the door carrying a cane and then walk toward the crowd with a limp. After the crowd sees Willy Wonka is a cripple, they all whisper to themselves and become deathly quiet. As I walk toward them, my cane sinks into one of the cobblestones I'm walking on and stands straight up, by itself; but I keep on walking until I realize that I no longer have my cane. I start to fall forward and just before I hit the ground, I do a beautiful forward somersault and bounce back up, to great applause." The scene was important to him, he said, because "from that time on, no one will know if I'm lying or telling the truth."

Wonka. Or *Wonky*?

Some of you are holding this book and I just used a word that nails exactly how you feel about the Church, and maybe about Christians in general. Some of you were given this book by a Christian who is well-intentioned but still a little strange from your perspective and this word perfectly describes what you feel about him or her or the church they attend. You don't have a problem with Jesus necessarily. It's the people that claim to follow him that you don't understand. Or can't stand. They're wonky.

I've been a pastor now for almost twenty years. I've worked in five different churches in three different states, and in every one of those places I have had meetings or moments where I found myself thinking, "Is there a good word to describe the chaos that is the church?" Yes, there is, and it's *wonky*.

I know. Kind of strange. Kind of funny. But apt.

Whether it was handling a conflict with someone who demanded I have the church building open for them earlier on Sundays because they gave the money that paid the bills in that holy building, or the people I thought hated me who suddenly became my best friends the day I announced my family and I were leaving the church, or the roller coaster of those transformed by the work of Jesus who quit coming to church the next week because life is too busy... the word wonky is a perfect fit.

Wonka. Wonky. One letter difference. I don't know if that was intentional by Roald Dahl, the author of the Willy Wonka stories for children, but it definitely could have been. Dahl was sorta, well, wonky himself. But I love the word wonky simply because it says what it feels. If you look up a definition for the word, it's simple: "crooked; off-center; askew." Or, "not functioning correctly; faulty."

When Willy Wonka walks out that red carpet so frail and decrepit before the second act of the original film, and then tumbles forward into the authenticity of his character, it's wonky. There's no other way to see him. Our view of him and of the entire film changes in that moment. Things get a little shaky. Our perspective changes. Suddenly, we're on our toes and wondering what's coming next – a little girl blowing up into a blueberry, a spoiled brat funneled into a trash compactor and facing incineration, a gluttonous boy sucked through a chocolate pipe, and a TV-addict loudmouth shrunken by his own obsession. Nothing is functioning correctly. Everything is off-center. The magical joy that came with the golden ticket is replaced by an unsteadiness that demands our full attention. Wonky indeed.

The Golden Ticket

Do you remember what it was like when you crossed the line of faith and became a follower of Jesus Christ? Do you remember the moment, or the journey, you took toward entering the Kingdom of God? I do. I was twelve years old and spending a week at a camp somewhere in the mountains of West Virginia. I spent four days listening to speakers, reading the Scriptures, and experiencing adults tell me the story of how much God loved me and wanted a personal relationship with me. At the end of that week, after one of the evening services, I remember retreating to the upstairs attic of one of the cabins where I knelt down and asked Jesus to live in my heart. I wanted to be a part of that story. I wanted to be saved.

And on that night, in that attic, I remember walking from the cabin down to the campfire and looking up at the stars and feeling better than Charlie Bucket finding the golden ticket. I felt like I'd been invited into the greatest adventure of my life.

I left camp with a new perspective. I fell in love not only with Jesus, but with his people. Church became my place and the people of the church became my tribe. The youth ministry I was a part of felt like home. I found a way to belong and grow and began to seek Jesus on my own. Over the next several years I was a church camp junkie. I traveled to the same West Virginia camp several times. I attended camps out of state. I served as a leader at camps. I went to South Africa for three weeks on a mission trip and felt God break my heart for the people around me and call me into full-time ministry. I attended a small Christian college and studied youth ministry, and then went home to lead the youth in my church in West Virginia. And that's when things got wonky.

> "THE CHURCH IS A WHORE.
> BUT SHE IS ALSO MY MOTHER."
> - DOROTHY DAY

I was only a part-time staff member, but I loved what I was doing as a job. But if you asked me if I loved every minute of it, I'd have to say no. Some of the people who had initially told me the loving story of Jesus were now acting and speaking in ways that were not so loving. There were interactions with leaders that left me hurting and frustrated and angry. Strong relationships unraveled. People got mad and left the church. There were emotions. Lots and lots of emotions.

That quote about the church? Yeah, we're not quite sure who said it. I'm actually pretty sure it wasn't Homer Simpson. Still, for the past sixteen years of my life, as I've served on the staff of multiple churches of various sizes in different contexts, I've felt that statement in the core of my bones. You see, for me, and for so many of you I would imagine, the church is the most magical place on the planet. I don't mean church buildings. I mean the people of God drawn together by the presence of the Holy Spirit and the person of Jesus Christ. I mean the people living the mission of God together. I still wake up every Sunday morning eager and grateful to gather with friends and have the immense privilege of sharing the Story of God with them as it relates to their lives. That golden ticket magic? It's never gone away for me. It is wondrous, like the warmth of a mother's love.

But sometimes, momma's not so pretty. I also know deeply the pain the Church can cause. I know friends who have rejected Jesus not because of Jesus, but because of his people and what they can be like. I know my own hurts. I know my own inability to trust others because of past pain. I know the longing of looking for a mentor who won't let you down only to find dry cisterns. I know what it means to shed tears over the house of God because of the flawed people of God—of who I am (if I can quote the Apostle Paul) the worst.

It's common today when I'm scrolling social media to find criticism after criticism of how the people of God – the Church – are failing. Many of my Christian friends are the greatest critics of the Church. And many times, rightfully so. In recent days I've scanned the news to see the sexual abuse scandal that is still sending shockwaves through the Catholic church. I watched a film preview telling a story about how fundamentalist Christians abusively tried to reorient a homosexual young man. I saw an article showing study results of how one entire wing of theology has a stronger bias toward believing domestic violence myths. I see certain political leaders continually attempting to co-opt the mission of Jesus as propaganda for their political world views. The Church is not held in the best light right now.

For the past twenty plus years, I've witnessed the people of God functioning as the Church be...
Fun.
Beautiful.
Strange.
Hurtful.
Incredible.
Awkward.
Broken.
Messy.
Ugly.
Taste of heaven.
Flavor of hell.
In other words, *wonky*.

Still My (Wonky) Mother

But here's the thing. I think that quote about the Church as a whore and our mother— whoever said it—is right on the money. Eight and a half years ago, I moved back to my hometown to start a brand-new church because I was tired of being cynical and critical. Yes, the church is a whore. But she's still my mother, and nobody gets to talk about my mom (even me) without me doing something about it. I was tired of complaining and having little to no ability or action to back up my criticisms. So, my wife Carrie and I started a church. We left a secure job in a growing church and moved back home to try to launch something from the ground up. And most of the time, if I'm honest, I feel like the frail Willy Wonka trying to hold myself up. But, at other times, I feel like I'm bringing joy to hundreds of others because of the amazing beauty of how God works through his people. It's messy. It's imperfect and flawed. It's wonky. But man, what an adventure!

So, I'm writing *Wonky* for those who haven't given up on the Church.

Wonky is for those who believe the bride of Christ is still the bride.

Wonky is for those who aren't living in denial about the imperfections of the church – oh we can be ugly!

Wonky is for those who are more convinced than ever that our world—our increasingly more political, cynical, critical, antagonistic, and divided world—now more than ever needs the true and beautiful Church to shine like the bride that it is.

Wonky is a walk through the church factory with honesty and authenticity.

Wonky is a survival guide for those who aren't ready to give up on the Church but wouldn't mind seeing it reimagined (can you hear Willy singing "Pure Imagination"?).

In the stories of *Wonky* I will share the chaos of emotions that come with being a part of any faith community, as well as the hope of redemption that floods those same emotions.

Wonky confronts the reality of anger and division in the Church.

Wonky examines the pain and hypocrisy that goes with chasing those away who only long to belong.

Wonky speaks of our own greed and pride and the failures of leadership and the heartbreak of broken relationships and racial division and sexual judgment and so much more.

And *Wonky* seeks a path toward beauty—a path where the communion of saints is truly that, a communion of broken sinners made whole by the mosaic of God's love.

I wrote *Wonky* for the people I've met who told me the body of Christ no longer felt safe.

I wrote *Wonky* for the people I hurt along the way in my years of ministry—the teens I judged, the parents I didn't encourage, the singles who felt too lonely after my teaching. I'm sorry for the hurt.

I wrote *Wonky* for those who, every once in a while, still remember the magic and wonder of the faith community and wish they could find a way back.

I wrote *Wonky* because I wanted to stop criticizing and start creating.

If you've been wounded by the church, chased away from Jesus by Christians, condemned with judgment from the eyes of the supposedly faithful, perhaps this book can be our coffee and conversation. Perhaps you'll find something here that serves as a salve to your wounds and helps remove the barrier that the church can often be between the wounded and the Healer. In these pages, I pray you'll find hope. I pray you'll find grace. I pray you'll find wisdom. And more than anything, I pray you'll find a love for the body of Christ—the Church—that births creative hope for the future of God's people.

One

Tiger Beat Pastors

Let's start on some common ground. We've all had miserable church encounters. And all too often, the misery of those experiences has come through actions of men just like me - those strange, mysterious, and threatening creatures that you call "the pastor" (insert your favorite scary music here).

At one of the churches where I was employed, I sat in a leadership meeting where for several months we had been discussing the split between our two worship services on Sunday mornings. One of the services involved a more traditional style of music which drew an older congregation, while the other was band-led and much more progressive, targeting a younger demographic. Because of the stylistic differences, the audiences for these services were very different, and often very divided. The pastor, who wanted to lead the church increasingly toward the more modern style, was simply enduring the traditional service until he could implement the changes he wanted to see. After several meetings with our staff discussing this, the pastor entered this meeting with a clear and decisive plan.

He walked boldly into our meeting room, approached the whiteboard, and wrote the following words in quotes:

"OPERATION: Aw-Shucks"

He then proceeded to tell us a long and involved story about his grandmother who was facing down Alzheimer's. As she aged, she was becoming more forgetful, more confused, and more disoriented. According to the pastor of this church, he and his extended family had taken an "Aw-Shucks!" approach to dealing with grandma. Their plan was simple— when grandma spoke nonsense, the family would "Aw-shucks" her until the moment passed and life moved on.

In regard to the divided worship services in our church, the pastor told us the way forward wasn't to keep fighting with "grandma," but simply put up with her until she was gone. When the traditional folks in our church didn't or couldn't understand the importance of his progressive vision for the future, we were to just "Aw-shucks" them.

I walked home from church that day mortified. I told my wife this pastor wouldn't last the year as the leader of that church. And about six weeks later, he was fired. *Aw-shucks.*

Wonky Leaders

Over the course of this book you'll find several strong statements I make about the nature of the church as a whole. You can consider these my confessions—things I've learned, seen, and noticed that are just plain wonky if we really think about them. Here's the first one:

One of the wonkiest parts of church-world continues to be the leadership of churches.

You have friends and I have friends who have been hurt deeply by a pastor. Many have been hurt by their own pastors. Leaders who have known them personally, known their families through pain and joy for many years, and somewhere along the line, these leaders (and they are most often men) have caused deep wounds. Chances are you yourself have been hurt by a pastor. I have been hurt by pastors. I have been the pastor who causes the hurt. It would not take much effort to dig out these stories.

William Willimon delineates the work of pastors as unique because, "a pastor can take initiative and intrude into the troubled lives of his or her people". Because of this, Willimon says:

> *A minister must not stay till he be sent for; but, of his own accord and care, go to them, to examine them, to exhort them to perfect their repentance, to strengthen their faith, to encourage their patience, to persuade them to resignation, to the renewing of their holy vows, to the love of God, to be reconciled to their neighbours, to make restitution and amends.[1]*

I've been told I agitate people as a pastor. A friend joked that my pursuit of him to live into the life Jesus had for him was as aggressive as Liam Neeson in the Taken films (I hope it was a joke!). So, I get what Willimon says. The work of pastoral ministry is a work of intrusion, of disturbing the peace for the sake of the kingdom. It is a work of calling others to their own calling.

But our reality of pastors hasn't matched up with that definition. Pastors have hurt us in a multitude of ways. Rather than kingdom disturbance and holy intrusion, oftentimes we simply find them disturbing. They've misused their power and authority. They've misappropriated money. They've failed morally. They've sacrificed their own families for the sake of growing (or what appear to be growing) ministries. They have held up standards of faith that they as individuals could not even abide. They didn't do enough. Or they did too much. Or they didn't do anything at all.

And so, for many of us, when the hurt just hurts too much, we check out of church because we are convinced that if the very leaders—the pastors of these churches—are nothing but hypocrites then why would we want anything to do with this church? But there's more to the pastor problem than just hurt.

Tiger Beat Pastors

Tiger Beat magazine. Does that ring any mental bells? *Tiger Beat* was the first of many teeny-bopper magazines aimed directly at teenagers. The magazine's mission? To capitalize on the fast sensation that is teen pop stars and one-hit wonders by sharing attractive pictures and loads of gossip about the lives of these stars. And all this, of course, to sell a ton of magazines. One writer simply described the celebrities featured in these magazines as "guys in their 20's singing 'La La' songs to 13-year old girls." (No better descriptor of boy-band mania has ever been penned.)

In many ways, the flip side of hypocritical leadership in churches today is what I call Tiger Beat Pastors. These pastors have more social media followers than many Hollywood celebrities. They lead churches whose weekly podcasts garner more followers than many of the series being produced by major media corporations like NPR. These charismatic, usually attractive, leaders have built congregations topping ten, twenty, even thirty thousand members.

With this said, if we are starting our exploration of the church and its wonky leadership by exploring pastor problems, let's be fair. The people in the pews (or the theater seats) often put too much stock and fixation on their pastors as the celebrities of their church. I'm not saying it's the same shallow fixation as middle school girls and boys with rising pop stars, but I am saying the same low maturity level of spirituality permeates the lives of many Christians when it comes to their perspectives of the leaders in their churches. Our obsession with pastor-so-and-so as the theological expert to tell us what we should believe and give us all the answers in every area of life is a blatant problem if we are simply consuming the leader's way of thinking without thinking for ourselves.

This rationale might create for us a spectrum of observing leadership within the church. On the one end we have the hurts and the wounds caused by actions of hypocritical leadership. At the other extreme of this spectrum is an almost celebrity-like worship of those leaders with the most charm, the hippest clothing, the coolest teaching, and the biggest production budget.

Building a Survival Guide

If we're going to build a survival guide for the wonky parts for following Jesus when you hate the church, we have to come to a healthy and mature understanding of what pastoral leadership in the church is truly all about. As with so many elements of our current culture, the problem is less with what pastoral leadership is today and more with what we have made it out to be. We must come to grips with the faults of our pastors *and* the faults of our expectations or assumptions about our pastors.

So, here's the good news. Well, maybe good news. **The Church has always had leadership issues.** From that Pentecost moment in the first century, the Church has struggled to understand healthy, biblical leadership. I call that good news because it shows we're not any more screwed up than those first disciples or any other church throughout the history of God's people. I guess the bad news is we're still just as screwed up.

Wonky Leadership in First Century Las Vegas

My approach in *Wonky* is to present several in-depth examples of the early Church in the years immediately following Jesus' death and resurrection. In these stories, I believe we find both comfort and counsel. Comfort, in the sense that the early Church often appears just as messy as the modern. And counsel, in the sense that it is still close to the time of Jesus and therefore perhaps closer to his original vision of the Church as it could be. Theologians call these discussions matters of ecclesiology. I call them the wonkiness of church life. If the problem for you isn't Jesus but his people, perhaps these snapshots of the early Church will press you beyond the versions you see today to the original and potent force of the people of God as they were originally intended and inspired by Jesus himself.

A combination of modern-day Las Vegas and New York City—that's how the first century Greco-Roman city of Corinth has been described. Corinth was eclectic, massively diverse, and amazingly busy. It is also where the Apostle Paul, arguably the greatest evangelist and church planter in history, shepherded one of the very first churches toward health. And one the first issues Paul had to deal with? You guessed it. Wonky leadership.

Paul's opening comments to the Corinthian church are anything but easy, no matter what church and in what age they are addressed to. He says this:

"I APPEAL TO YOU, BROTHERS AND SISTERS, IN THE NAME OF OUR LORD JESUS CHRIST, THAT ALL OF YOU AGREE WITH ONE ANOTHER IN WHAT YOU SAY AND THAT THERE BE NO DIVISIONS AMONG YOU, BUT THAT YOU BE PERFECTLY UNITED IN MIND AND THOUGHT."

(1 COR. 1:10)

Now, I have to tell you, part of me wants to close this file and quit writing simply because this command of Paul seems so monstrously impossible based on what I know about every church I have ever served. ALL of you agree? NO divisions? PERFECTLY UNITED? C'mon, Paul, are you kidding me? Have you read about the 2020 election and how divided churches were and are? But it doesn't stop there. Paul presses on with a specific example of the divisions.

> "MY BROTHERS AND SISTERS, SOME FROM CHLOE'S HOUSEHOLD HAVE INFORMED ME THAT THERE ARE QUARRELS AMONG YOU. WHAT I MEAN IS THIS: ONE OF YOU SAYS, 'I FOLLOW PAUL'; ANOTHER, 'I FOLLOW APOLLOS'; ANOTHER, 'I FOLLOW CEPHAS'; STILL ANOTHER, 'I FOLLOW CHRIST.'"
>
> (1 COR. 1:11-12)

In his first letter to the Corinthians, Paul addresses eleven specific issues. Now, check this out. *Ten of them have absolutely nothing to do with theology.* Not a thing. Those ten pertain to practical, specific, directly life-related issues. And the first and largest section of these issues deals specifically with church leadership. They didn't know it, but the Corinthians had a serious Tiger Beat culture going on.

In the Corinthian culture, leadership wasn't something attributed to people who were of noble character or admirable talent. Instead, the Corinthian culture based the influence of leaders on their cultural status - and status could be gained if you knew how to work the system. Think social media in the ancient world. Can you say *influencers*?

Class systems owned the day. If you were of noble birth or born free and wealthy, you had a leg up in this honor culture system.

However, it didn't necessarily end your chances if you didn't have the right credentials. In fact, you could often buy influence. It was common for the wealthy in Corinth to offer financial gifts to those of lower status. If those given the gifts could return a gift of equal value this implied equality in friendship. If they could not afford a gift, though, they were then indebted as a "patron" of the one who had originally given the gift. What this often created in the town square was scenes of patrons and their followers, vying passionately for the attention and the influence of those who needed a leader to follow. (It was also not uncommon for those longing for influence to go into massive debt trying to buy the status they wanted. Sound familiar?) Along with this, Corinth—like most of the Greco-Roman world—celebrated the oratory gifts. Those who could speak and speak well, those who could argue, those who could philosophize, these were the influential ones in a city looking for the best public speakers.

So, picture this. You show up to the gathering spot in the city, perhaps a marketplace type of town square where goods are traded and people commonly gather. You show up and hear loud, boisterous arguments. You look and see two wealthy-looking Corinthian men passionately debating the latest political climate. And directly behind each of them stand a small group of followers—their patrons— cheering them on from their own indebtedness and hoping that if their chosen leader wins this speaking contest they too might begin the ascent of the social ladder.

It is this culture to which Paul writes of the quarrels affecting the Corinthian church, calling out their divisive hearts over following Paul, Apollos, Peter, and even Christ himself. He is staring down the Corinthian church and letting them know they have become no different than the broader patron-client culture around them. It is this culture to which Paul makes his next point so clear:

"IS CHRIST DIVIDED? WAS PAUL CRUCIFIED FOR YOU?..."

(1 COR. 1:13)

WONKY CHURCH SURVIVAL TIP #1:
FOCUS ON JESUS MORE THAN YOUR PASTOR.

We live in a celebrity-obsessed culture. We are not that much different than the city of Corinth. Our language on social media even celebrates the numbers of followers we gain. We have apps built to gain more followers, track our number of followers, tell us when we lose followers. And all of us have someone (or multiple someones) that we LOVE to follow. People we look up to. Emulate. Admire. Respect. Retweet. And these are all fine things and possibly fine people, if they are held in their rightful place. But this becomes problematic when this celebrity-follower culture permeates the way we assume life in the church should be.

Jesus Wasn't Pretty

You know what's fascinating?

If Jesus had a Twitter account, I don't think he would have that many followers. I don't think his Instagram feed would be blowing up with likes. I don't think his YouTube videos would go viral. And, I'm pretty sure if Jesus had pastored a church it wouldn't be noted on the list of Israel's "fastest growing churches." And actually, I believe these assumptions I'm making are biblically-based.

In Isaiah 53, the prophet paints a picture of the Savior that would come so many hundreds of years later—a portrait of what is known as the "Suffering Servant." The prophecy of Jesus is about his suffering, his rejection, and his willingness to experience the depths of pain on our behalf. But right in the middle of this prophecy is this simple statement about the coming Savior:

"HE HAD NO BEAUTY OR MAJESTY TO ATTRACT US TO HIM, NOTHING IN HIS APPEARANCE THAT WE SHOULD DESIRE HIM. HE WAS DESPISED AND REJECTED BY MANKIND... LIKE ONE FROM WHOM PEOPLE HIDE THEIR FACES HE WAS DESPISED, AND WE HELD HIM IN LOW ESTEEM." (ISAIAH 53:2, 3)

This blows my mind in the midst of our Tiger Beat culture. God is about to send a Savior to his people, a messenger and a Messiah to call people back to himself, and we are told he's not going to be someone that we'll really be drawn to. This teaches us something about the nature of following Jesus. It has never been about celebrity-status, outward appearance, amazing production quality, or super-famous pastors. No, the way of Jesus has always been about a leader who emptied himself and suffered for the sake of a people who were lost, and a call for his followers to be willing to do the same.

Paul's Own Story of Calling

Paul continues in the second chapter of 1 Corinthians this conversation about the division over leaders by telling his own story.

"WHEN I CAME TO YOU, I DID NOT COME WITH ELOQUENCE OR HUMAN WISDOM... FOR I RESOLVED TO NOTHING WHILE I WAS WITH YOU

EXCEPT JESUS CHRIST AND HIM CRUCIFIED. I CAME TO YOU IN WEAK-NESS WITH GREAT FEAR AND TREMBLING. MY MESSAGE AND MY PREACHING WERE NOT WITH WISE AND PERSUASIVE WORDS, BUT WITH A DEMONSTRATION OF THE SPIRIT'S POWER, SO THAT YOUR FAITH MIGHT NOT REST ON HUMAN WISDOM, BUT ON GOD'S POWER."

(1 COR. 2:1-5)

I don't know if Paul hurt people with his leadership. I don't know if he ever made any hypocritical decisions. He was human, so I have to think he did. I do know that

Paul never forgot his own story, and that kept him humble.

These verses show a leader who was about as counter-Corinthian as you could be. He wasn't trying to gain more clients in the patron-client system. He wasn't trying to prove his status through smoothly crafted words. He wasn't looking to build his congregational numbers. He was simply reminding the people of this church of his own broken nature as a human being. He tells them he didn't come with "eloquence" or "human wisdom," and he came with "great fear and trembling." These are the words of someone who remembers what it means to start from nowhere and be rescued by Jesus. And that leads to the second survival tip:

WONKY CHURCH SURVIVAL TIP #2:
EVERY LEADER HAS A STORY.
DON'T EVER FOLLOW A LEADER WHO HAS FORGOTTEN
HIS OR HER STORY.

I believe that the most hypocritical church leaders I've known—the ones who have hurt me deeply— did not set out with the intent of being hypocritical. In fact, the leaders who have hurt me the most still stand as spiritual giants in my life because of the power of their personal faith stories. But the breakdown of their leadership and the beginning of the pain they inflicted began the moment they forgot their own story. Arrogance is never your pastor's end goal. But it can happen over time in the midst of a celebrity culture. I talk often with my wife about the fact that I don't want to forget my story. I don't want to forget that as a boy I would hide shyly behind my mother's legs, and now I stand before crowds every week trying the best I can to proclaim hope and truth in Jesus. I don't want to forget that I have always wondered where I fit in, if I measure up, if I'll ever be good enough, if I can ever do enough. I don't want to forget that in the midst of those uncertainties Jesus persistently shows up to say, "*I am enough even if you aren't.*" This is my story; and for me, it's powerful. I don't want to ever forget.

For those of you who have been hurt deeply by your pastor or leader, I'm sorry. I'm sorry for what happened. I'm sorry if there was abuse, any kind of abuse. I'm sorry for the lies. I'm sorry for the wounds. I'm truly sorry. I also want to say those leaders don't represent all leaders, they don't represent Jesus, and it's okay to get out of toxic situations. If your spiritual leader has forgotten his or her story, he or she is no longer worth following.

Breastfeeding in the Front Row

"…I COULD NOT ADDRESS YOU AS PEOPLE WHO LIVE BY THE SPIRIT BUT AS PEOPLE WHO ARE STILL WORLDLY—MERE INFANTS IN CHRIST. I GAVE YOU MILK, NOT SOLID FOOD, FOR YOU WERE NOT READY FOR IT.

INDEED YOU ARE STILL NOT READY. YOU ARE STILL WORLDLY."

(1 COR. 3:1-3)

A few years ago, a friend told me a story of one of the most awkward moments I've ever heard of in a church. The pastor—a 40-something year-old man—was preaching and well into his text for the morning. His wife, a faithful and attentive servant of the church, sat quietly on the front row. About halfway through the sermon, the couple's child (3 or 4 years old) walked to where his mother was sitting and said loudly enough for the congregation to hear, "Mommy, I'm hungry."

No big deal, right? Happens all the time. Hungry children in church. Mom has some crackers or cookies. Except instead of crackers or cookies, the pastor's wife unhitched her shirt and proceeded to breastfeed the child until he told her he was finished. Wonky, right? But also a powerful illustration. When Paul tells these Corinthian believers that he can't even give them solid food yet, he is calling out another of their problems with the leadership issues facing the church. Paul makes it clear that these issues have less to do with the spiritual authority of the leaders and more to do with the spiritual maturity of the believers.

> **WONKY CHURCH SURVIVAL TIP #3:**
> **STOP NURSING FROM YOUR LEADERS WHEN**
> **YOU'RE INVITED TO FEAST WITH A KING.**

Paul tells the Corinthians that they're missing the feast. They're longing for more and more spiritual milk - intended for babies - and missing out on the meat. Every time they argue over following Paul or Peter or Apollos, they're returning to their nursing station and missing the fact that Christ has never been divided and he's always offered an invitation to the richest feast the world has ever known.

While I have a great deal of compassion for those who have been hurt by the hypocrisy of poor Christian leadership, I have little sympathy for those who refuse to mature in their faith. There is rarely a week that goes by that I don't hear of divisions in the church that are caused by nothing other than spiritual immaturity.

What's a Pastor Anyway?

Paul keeps rolling in the third chapter of this letter to the Corinthians by picking apart one of their favorite leaders – Apollos – and himself:

> "WHAT, AFTER ALL, IS APOLLOS? AND WHAT IS PAUL? ONLY SER-
> VANTS, THROUGH WHOM YOU CAME TO BELIEVE—AS THE LORD HAS AS-
> SIGNED TO EACH HIS TASK. I PLANTED THE SEED, APOLLOS WATERED
> IT, BUT GOD HAS BEEN MAKING IT GROW… FOR WE ARE CO-WORKERS IN
> GOD'S SERVICE; YOU ARE GOD'S FIELD, GOD'S BUILDING."
>
> (1 COR. 3:5-6, 9)

In these verses, Paul questions the very worth of what it means to be considered credible. "What, after all, are we?" asks Paul. His conclusion: We are simply co-workers. The people are God's field, God's building; therefore, perhaps Paul planted a seed and Apollos watered it, but the growth and the fruitfulness all come down to the work of God himself.

Maybe you've lived through ministries with leaders who were *all control all the time.* Maybe you've experienced pastoral ministry that felt more like you were a cog and the pastor's church was the machine full of steps and systems and programs and processes What I'd like to suggest to you is that this type of leadership has nothing to do with God's intended design and intentional call for pastoral ministry. Paul's language here is all about the true nature of pastoral ministry: cultivation rather than control.

Cultivation is a powerful metaphor for pastoral ministry. It suggests that all the materials, all the resources necessary for growth, are already in existence. Christian leaders who understand cultivation never forget their stories because they are constantly living into the present story God's Spirit is working in them. Leaders who cultivate aren't afraid to get their hands dirty and immerse themselves in understanding soil conditions and weather patterns and the needed preparation and ongoing pruning required for growth. Cultivation is ultimately about nurture. Cultivation is about care.

So Stop It

> "SO THEN, NO MORE BOASTING ABOUT HUMAN LEADERS! ALL THINGS ARE YOURS, WHETHER PAUL OR APOLLOS OR CEPHAS OR THE WORLD OR LIFE OR DEATH OR THE PRESENT OR THE FUTURE—ALL ARE YOURS, AND YOU ARE OF CHRIST, AND CHRIST IS OF GOD."
>
> *(1 COR. 3:21-23)*

This is where Paul loses his patience. This is where his sermon starts elevating in tone and he might start to shout a bit. He builds his argument to this climax and just blurts it out, "STOP IT!" Stop living like the rest of your city boasting about your leaders and showing off your Tiger Beat obsessions over your favorite preachers. "STOP IT!"

And then he follows his rant with this simple phrase: "All things are yours." Whether it's Paul or Apollos or Cephas or whether it's life or death or present or future... "All things are yours."

Paul is continuing to confront the lack of maturity in the Corinthian church. He's calling out their Tiger Beat culture and saying their teeny-bopper views of the world are no place to get the truth about life. If they are going to be self-feeding disciples who make disciples—obedient to the commission of Christ—then they're going to be growing spiritually wherever they can. It's all there for them (and us) to grow. Paul, Apollos, Cephas, pastor-so-and-so... they are all signposts pointing to Jesus. All things are yours. This means at the root of your existence—if you are a follower of Christ—you have a responsibility and ownership of your spiritual discipleship.

Confessions of a Pastor

I have always struggled with the label "pastor." It just kind of gives me the heebie-jeebies. In some congregations where I've preached it's like the congregation thought my first name was Pastor and my middle name was Justin. I'm always grateful that the church we planted doesn't reference me in just that way. I don't know what it was, but that title just seemed to create a divide between myself and the people I was leading.

But over the years I've found a gentle acceptance of the word "pastor" when placed with my name. I've found God using this title to define my call. This gentle acceptance has come as I've allowed the word Paul used to define himself to define my role as pastor. He says this in closing this section of his letter:

> "THIS, THEN, IS HOW YOU OUGHT TO REGARD US: AS SERVANTS OF CHRIST..."
>
> (1 COR. 4:1)

There's the word—"servant." The acceptance I've found for being called pastor is rooted in the privilege I feel serving the people of God. It is an honor to try—failing miserably at times—to pour myself out for people who are finding their identity as the sons and daughters of Christ. I would love to tell you in my ministry career that I've never hurt anyone in the way that you have perhaps been hurt. I would love to tell you that, but I can't. What I will tell you is that I recognize the hurt I have caused, and even today it still haunts me.

I remember teaching a group of students regarding the subject of dating and spending time dealing with Biblical modesty. I remember a group of those high school girls feeling so uncomfortable that they never returned to church. That was my fault.

I remember leaving one ministry position and having a student so broken-hearted that our relationship with him was ending that he was never the same. Years later I can still find him on social media publicly scorning any semblance of the Christian faith. In many ways, that was my fault.

I remember pouring countless hours into a student, counseling and listening, leading and directing, only to have her make choices in her twenties that would crush many of the relationships in her life. I remember her sitting hungover in our house looking for answers and feeling only frustration for her repeatedly bad decisions. Today, I don't think she's walking with Christ. I feel like that was my fault.

I have been hurt, yes. But I've also caused the hurt. And if I could, even today I would love to talk with each of these individuals and ask for their forgiveness and potentially be a catalyst for healing in their lives. Not because I want them to love me, but simply because I don't want to stand in the way of their relationship with Jesus.

In one case, in one of these stories, I did reach out and asked the student for his forgiveness. I told him if he ever wanted to talk, I would love that. And I heard absolutely nothing.

I hope your hurt isn't beyond healing. I'm praying you find hope. Maybe here you find a reminder that you too, have a story. Maybe you find a whisper that your story isn't over; and while that leader who misrepresented Jesus to you failed miserably, that leader was never meant to replace Jesus and Jesus has never gone away. You see the thing is, even amidst my failures, in all of these stories and in all of these lives I just recounted, it was still a joy to SERVE them. It is a joy to tell the story of Good News to them. It was, and is, an honor to be their pastor.

[1] Willimon, *Pastor: The Theology and Practice of Ordained Ministry*. Nashville, Abingdon Press, 2016.

Two

Defining the Relationship

When I originally thought about writing *Wonky*, I posted a question on social media asking my own network to share just exactly how they had experienced hurt, pain, embarrassment, or just the overall chaos that can happen in churches. The responses blew me away. Of course, there were a few humorous stories, but the majority were heartbreaking accounts of people being asked to leave churches based on different opinions about everything from clothing styles to lifestyle choices. And as you might guess, there were stories of politics superseding theology and mission. But you know what surprised me more than the nature of the responses? The speed of the responses. Almost as soon as the post went up, I saw comments and stories coming in. People felt the pain of churches, but they felt the pain strongly and they *needed* to get it out. It was visceral, like purging themselves of these stories was cathartic for these people. I can only imagine the stories that were too painful to share publicly. Watching the responses roll in was like watching my friends go through a bad breakup.

Do you remember that commercial where the girl is breaking up with her boyfriend and she's chucking his stuff out of their apartment window? I don't remember what the commercial was advertising, I just remember this guy's stuff being thrown out the window. She's angry. A TV comes crashing to the pavement. She tears a picture apart, and the next thing you know his guitar shatters in a thousand pieces. She's purging herself of all the pain he's caused. Maybe you've been there. Maybe you've thrown something, torn stuff, or destroyed things that belonged to your significant other just so you could feel a little bit better. Maybe you were with someone for a while and when it ended, it ended badly. Maybe you didn't know what to do with all the emotions at that point—the anger and frustration and hurt and sadness. So you took action by going on the offensive. Maybe you burned things or blasted him or her on social media or held his dog hostage and demanded a ransom. Whatever it was you did or said, the result was a purging, moving the things inside you to the outside.

But there's something about those purging moments that have always caused a bit of a disconnect for me. Take, for instance, that commercial. Watching that commercial and seeing that woman who is clearly justified in tossing the memories out the window, all I can feel is sympathy for the very nice guitar shattered on the sidewalk below. I understand she's hurt, and I understand her actions, but I still feel for the guitar. I mean, that guitar didn't do anything to deserve being smashed like that. I get it. We get hurt and mad and we need *somewhere* or *something* to absorb that pain. But all too often we're taking our pain out on the wrong things because we can't take it out on the right things. When it comes to the pain we've all felt from wonky church experiences, a good deal of that pain comes from having invested our emotions in a central relationship that was never meant to be central. It's what some spiritual writers refer to as "disordered affections."

Relational Webs

Spider webs are fascinating. They are composed of silk that is produced in the glands of a spider's spinnerets. When spiders decide what type of web to make, they can choose silk threads that are thick, thin, dry, sticky, beaded, or smooth. This silk begins as a liquid but dries quickly in the fresh air. To form the web, a spider anchors its thread to something solid - a branch, a corner of a room, or a doorframe. Then, as it begins to move back and forth, adding threads, the spider creates a unique pattern and strengthens the web.

Now here's where I think it gets really interesting. Spider webs can actually survive hurricane-force winds. They are actually stronger than steel, a strength that comes from the design of the web. When a single strand breaks, the strength of the web actually increases because the tension shifts to other elements of the web. Put simply, for the web to fall apart multiple strands would need to be broken, including the anchor point. As a spider web stands, the destruction of one thread barely affects the rest of the web. I believe our relationships have the same potential for strength as spider webs.

Every single one of us live our daily existence in the middle of several relational webs. We are connected to other people in multiple ways and at multiple levels. Sure, some relationships are stronger than others, but the fact is we are all connected. If you're married, your relational web to your husband or wife can and should be the strongest connection you experience. We also have strong relational connections to our children. The joys and the challenges they bring to our lives create a deep emotional bond that is undeniable. This is another part of our relational webs.

If we press further into our relational webs, we might find a thread connected to our extended family. In my context—the Appalachian culture—the extended family web is often very strong.

Aunts, uncles, grandparents, and others all form a deep connection in the relational life of individuals. Yet another strand in our relational webs can be connections to our broader community—our friends, co-workers, and neighbors. These webs remind us that we are formed and forged by our network of relationships. Each of us, as individuals, are incredibly influenced, guided, and guarded by our relational webs.

Yet here's the thing. Our relational webs (affections) are not always properly ordered (disordered). The reality is that many of us have our relational webs all out of whack. Some of you, if you're honest, might have to confess that your dog is often more relationally important than your spouse (ahem). Yeah, disordered affections.

For others, it may be a sports team, the way you spend your weekends, or the things you buy. The truth is when our relational webs are out of order and we begin to treat other, lesser relationships with more importance than our central essential relationships, problems are bound to emerge. What this out of order web creates is a weak web. It's like a spider anchoring its most important thread to a feather. It just won't hold up.

Faith Webs

For those who have encountered Jesus, somewhere along the line chances are your faith was somehow intertwined with a "church" experience of some kind. For me, I attended a church camp. This is where I placed my trust in Jesus. For others, it was a Vacation Bible School, a youth ministry, a college ministry, or some other type of ministry that opened a door for you to hear more about the Good News of Jesus. After you encountered Jesus in this way, chances are good you became connected to some kind of Christian community. This could be a church, a parachurch ministry, a house church, or simply a regular gathering of a small group of believers. If this holds up, this is a strong web. You build an anchor relationship with Jesus and because of that relationship you engage the faith community. Put simply—Jesus first and community second .

But here's where things can get a little messed up. Too often, and for a multitude of reasons, just like the disordered affections in our relational webs, the same thing happens in our faith web. Often, the more we engage in the life of the Christian community—through church programs, planning events, outreach programs, or whatever other well-intentioned efforts we could describe—we transfer our relationship (affection) with Jesus to a secondary role and place our relationship with the faith community—or church, or pastor, etc.—in a primary position. Yeah, disordered. And it is at this point that our faith web weakens and what was meant to be stronger than steel is now anchored to the weak and wonky nature of the Christian community.

Defining the Relationships

I started dating my wife Carrie when I was in high school. We skipped school one day (with parental approval) to go skiing. That evening, we watched a scary movie and I held her hand for the first time. It was magic. Then she freaked out and lost interest for a couple months. But I didn't give up. And just a few months later we were holding hands again. And I was thoroughly confused. So we stopped at KFC (it was still Kentucky Fried Chicken at this time) one day after school and had the DTR conversation. Do you remember DTR conversations? Defining the Relationship. We sat and had some honest conversation about whether or not we were dating and what we wanted from this relationship. I found out she did want to date me, and almost twenty-five years later, we're still together.

DTR conversations. They can be, like this one was for me, full of joy and excitement. They can also be painful and awkward, uncomfortable and uncertain. But if the relationship matters in any way, such conversations are essential and necessary, and usually don't happen accidentally. Intentionality is involved. As we continue to build a survival guide to follow Jesus and (maybe) even learn to love the wonky church, I want to invite you in this chapter to have a DTR conversation with Jesus. That's right. I want to invite you to intentionally and honestly assess the strength of your faith web.

> WONKY CHURCH SURVIVAL TIP #4:
> YOUR RELATIONSHIP WITH JESUS MUST BE STRONGER
> THAN YOUR RELATIONSHIP TO THE CHURCH.

A Story from the First Church

In the last chapter, we looked at the Corinthian church. We'll get back to Corinth in later chapters, but for now I want to take a detour to that first group of believers who were trying desperately to figure out what following Jesus looked like when Jesus was no longer on the earth. In the book of Acts, we find a thriving and mission-centered faith community of Christians who were also a little bit wonky themselves. They didn't know what this new way of believing meant for their life together, and the broader culture's system of religion was completely uncertain what to do with them. Let's consider one of the first wonky moments of this church.

In the book of Acts, chapter 3, Peter and John and the other followers who had been sharing life directly with Jesus performed a miraculous healing of a crippled beggar. The miracle happened just outside the Jewish Temple. Immediately after the healing, the writer says that the healed man "held on" to Peter and John where they stood. As you might expect, a crowd gathers, and the Temple guards and priests (think "religious police") approach Peter and John. This is what we're told at the start of Acts chapter 4:

"THEY WERE GREATLY DISTURBED BECAUSE THE APOSTLES WERE TEACHING THE PEOPLE, PROCLAIMING IN JESUS THE RESURRECTION OF THE DEAD."

(ACTS 4:2)

"Greatly disturbed." Because people are hearing about life after you die. Go figure. Now think about this, because it is wonkier than any church experience you've ever had. A man who has been crippled for years is healed in the name of Jesus, and the ones who performed the healing began to declare Jesus and the resurrection to the gathering crowd . And the literal, freaking religious police show up and try to shut it down. Wonky.

Remember, I'm inviting you to define your relationship with Jesus and who's first—Jesus or the church. As we look at the faith community that actually keeps the relationship with Jesus first, we see this as a key indicator: **Jesus is declared.**

Many of you no doubt grew up in Sunday School and Jesus was always the right answer, and this sounds like more of that. But don't brush past this because here's the reality. In many faith communities where I've seen people hurt deeply by the church, the relationship with the church supersedes the relationship with Jesus because life in Jesus is not being proclaimed.

I have served in churches where so many other things are declared. I was in a church once where the preacher taught for forty-five minutes about a parable that clearly pointed to the suffering, death, and resurrection of Jesus. But the central point of the sermon was why hard work is important. Go figure.

WONKY CHURCH SURVIVAL TIP #5:
FIND A FAITH COMMUNITY WHERE LIFE IN JESUS IS
CONSISTENTLY PROCLAIMED.

Maybe you're thinking "What else would a *church* proclaim besides Jesus?" Good question. But it's more common than you think. Churches all over our world today have removed Jesus from the central place of their vision and replaced him with other things that, while they are not innately bad, they are also not Jesus. See if any of this sounds familiar.

Have you ever been in a faith community where good works in the community took precedence over life in Jesus? What about a church where politics—whatever political perspective it might be—stood head and shoulders above Jesus? Or maybe you've seen the church where everything revolves around a feel-good theology that keeps everyone happy Then again, maybe you grew up in a setting where guilt, legalism, and religion reigned supreme. You see, all of these other elements can sit on the throne of our faith communities, and when this happens, we lose sight of the Savior. And we might as well be blind.

The thing is it is rarely intentional. I don't know of any churches who held a strategic meeting and decided, "We don't want to be about Jesus anymore." No one does that. No pastor does that. No elder team does that. But when that relationship (affection) gets out of order, it leaves our faith weak.

There's another side to this though. I believe if you sat down with Jesus and defined your relationship all over again, I believe there is something he would want you to know. I think there is something he would want you to notice about this story with Peter and John because it reveals a principle that we find throughout the New Testament: **Life in Jesus *always* means the death of religion.**

Do you know why the "religious police" showed up in the Temple? Do you know what caused the uproar? Peter and John declared that a man who had died had come back to life, and that Jesus had done this so that all the dying people who were hopeless and guilty in the Temple could be brought back to life as well. It was this message that totally enraged the religious guardians.

Within the Jewish religion there existed a clear system of moral legalism. Rules made life clear. If I failed to please God, I could simply find the Torah guidelines for getting back into good standing. Even today, I understand and sympathize with my legalistic brothers and sisters because if I can learn the rules, I'll know when I measure up and when I don't. In a legalistic system, grace always messes up the religious boundaries. Life in Jesus always kills religion. Always.

Surviving the Church Will Cost You

This story of Peter and John keeps moving. And the next part is a bit uncomfortable. The religious police arrest them. They put them in jail until the next day because it's too late for a trial. I say this is uncomfortable because it reveals something that is true of those who have a relationship with Jesus at the core of their faith web. The indicator of the Jesus-centered disciple is clear—suffering. I'm probably the worst church-marketer you can imagine. But I'm telling you, it's true. **The church that suffers has always been the strongest.**

I recently read an article where the author debated whether real persecution actually helps the church or not. The author said he wasn't convinced because persecution carries with it a tension (don't forget that word). He explained how at times, the church has functioned most clearly on mission when it was functioning under threat of persecution. In fact, the majority of movements that have offered real and lasting change in the world have thrived under persecution. Even now, the Chinese church is exploding with growth, and much of that is directly related to the persecution Chinese believers face.

For decades the Chinese government has persecuted religious minorities—including Christians. In 2013, President Xi took office and under his leadership the nation of China has intensified this persecution. One pastor refused to place government issued video cameras in their church and immediately faced threats of being kicked out of their building. Other stories involve abduction, rape, detainment in prison, amputation of limbs and even beheadings. Churches have gathered to meet only to find their crosses burned and Communist propaganda now replacing their sacred images. In other parts of the world, persecution looks like ethnic cleansing, terrorism, organized crime, and fear tactics designed to shatter the faith communities.

Let me be clear. When I talk about suffering as an indicator of the healthy church, I'm not talking about friends looking at you funny because you prayed before your lunch. I'm not talking about politicians who want to unhinge your religious liberties. I'm talking about real life or death persecution that enhances our faith in Christ.

But I told you there was a tension, didn't I? When the author of this article was interviewed, he also mentioned that persecution can kill a church. In Iraq, for instance, the church has transitioned from about 5% of the country's population to about 0.5% in the last 50 years. When asked about the differences between thriving in persecution and dying in persecution, the author said this:

"The difference is how far the church establishes itself among the mass of people and doesn't just become the church of a particular segment, a class or ethnic group ."[1]

That's a powerful statement because in many ways it describes what we hear today from the loudest and wonkiest Evangelical church voices. There is a rallying cry from certain American Evangelical leaders declaring that the freedoms of Christians are being taken away, and it is this cry that instills a pervasive sense of fear and anger. Historically and biblically-speaking, I'm not convinced the church of Jesus was ever supposed to be the mass majority of a society holding all the moral influence and power and authority. In fact, when this happens—time and time again—it seems to be the place where the missional momentum of the church begins to die.

If our faith communities only represent our own preferred ideologies, preferences, ethnicities, or demographics, we are missing the point. The author of this article continued, "When Christianity is at its weakest in one area, amazing new opportunities open elsewhere." So, when the Christian faith dies in the Middle East in 1915, it erupts like a fire in Africa. Even now, as we are watching the decline of North American influence on the global church, the global south including Africa and Latin and South America are thriving in missional endeavors.

It wouldn't be too much of a stretch for me to assume that the majority of you reading this book have never once experienced real and authentic persecution. But, and I know this is bold, if we are going to follow Jesus, then maybe we should experience this very thing called suffering for our faith. In fact, I believe real and authentic persecution might reorient us toward a faith that defines Jesus at the center of the relationship. Most of us have never truly suffered for Jesus—giving up coffee or chocolate for Lent doesn't count—but perhaps if we did it would cause us to cling to Jesus more than we grow frustrated with the church. We might get our affections in order.

A True Movement

"BUT MANY WHO HEARD THE MESSAGE BELIEVED; SO THE NUMBER OF MEN WHO BELIEVED GREW TO ABOUT FIVE THOUSAND."

(ACTS 4:4)

I love this because I believe it's another blatant reminder of what non-wonky (un-wonky) (healthy) Christian community really looks like. It's simple and profound at the same time, and I'd like to put it before you as a question: **In the faith community where you find yourself, are people who don't know Jesus regularly coming to Jesus?**

Eight and a half years ago, when my wife and I planted our church New Community, the most common question we heard in a rural West Virginia small-town with an already over-abundance of churches was, "Why do we need another church in this town?" It's a great question. And, as I used to answer these folks, I would tell them I may not have the best answer, but this is the answer that matters the most to me.

Somewhere along our church planting journey, the mom of one of our elementary kids in the church asked if I would talk with her daughter as she had some questions about Jesus. We sat down-- mom and little girl and I-- and began to chat one evening. The daughter didn't really know what to ask, she was very shy. So, I started telling her about Jesus and how much he loved her and how he had left heaven to come and make a way to have a relationship with her. We talked for a while and as we wrapped up I asked her if this made sense. The little girl (and her mom) both nodded. I asked them if they had ever made that story a true part of their lives and if they would like to follow Jesus. The little girl quickly nodded, and mom simply said, "Me too." This is why we need another church.

In 2009, only 15% of the population of West Virginia reported attending a church on Sundays. That means contrary to other popular opinions about how so many people are believers in the U.S., 85% of the people in our state were not in a church. If you keep studying these statistics, you find that in a new church plant somewhere between 60-80% of the church's membership comes from new conversions.[2] That means people who didn't know Jesus are coming to Jesus for the first time.

So, here's what I know. I don't mean this critically or arrogantly, but we are being honest about the wonkiness of churches, so here goes. If you're in a church, if you lead a church, if you're at all engaged in a church, too often we say we believe in the life, death, and resurrection of Jesus but our churches today are failing at calling people who don't know Jesus to a faith in Jesus. We are not offering frequently enough about an invitation to lost people to cross a line of faith and trust Jesus with all that they are. Only 52% of Christians shared their faith with someone of a different belief system in the past year; and 80% of Christians identify Christ as Savior before the age of 17. In many ways, we who lead the wonky churches have subtly removed Jesus from the center of our mission.

The reality is that every pastor, every congregant, and every church leader knows specifically the names and faces of non-Christians in their neighborhoods. We know them. We see them. You may be reading this and be one of them. I'm not trying to promote an us and them mentality, but I am saying that if we claim to be a part of a movement that believes in a Savior who conquered death and we're not creating churches that invite people to this conversion, we either don't know how or we simply don't care enough.

Can I speak directly to those of you who are a little bit wonky yourself? If you're not praying for, talking to, investing time with, and inviting your non-Christian friends to a place where they can hear and receive the hope of life in Jesus, but you still have a commitment to a church, then your relationship with Jesus and the church is like that out of whack spider web.

Tell AND Show

The story continues for Peter and John with a pivotal question:

> *"BY WHAT POWER OR WHAT NAME DID YOU DO THIS?"*
>
> *(ACTS 4:7)*

Peter and John are brought to question *because of* the power and healing that happened as a result of their relationship with Jesus. We can't miss this. In Acts 3, when this healing occurs, the crippled man isn't asking for healing. He doesn't ask Peter and John to heal him. He is actually a beggar on the street, looking for money. He wants resources. But check out Peter's response to his begging:

> *"SILVER OR GOLD I DO NOT HAVE, BUT WHAT I DO HAVE I GIVE YOU.*
> *IN THE NAME OF JESUS CHRIST OF NAZARETH, WALK."*
>
> *(ACTS 3:6)*

I find this one of the most beautiful pieces of Scripture in the entire Bible. We see a beggar looking for *resources* and the apostles gave him *rescue*. It is the mark of a church with Jesus at the center—healing and power are always displayed. In the church my wife and I planted, one of the ways I know God is doing good things is because so many folks in our congregation are sharing with me their stories of personal healing. So many men and women I know are making hard decisions to deal with emotional pain, to move out of the wounds of the past, to step in health away from brokenness. I literally had a counselor from our community tell me our church kept her in business. I love that because it means healing is happening.

For too long in church circles, debates have raged over whether the gospel should be primarily driven by proclamation (preaching the gospel) or demonstration (living and embodying the gospel). These debates have centered on those who insist preaching for conversion is the first order, while others claim if we do not do the work of justice and restoration (demonstration) there is no opportunity for conversion. As with so many elements in our polarized world, we must reclaim the power of both. Ed Stetzer, a leading missiologist, calls this "integral missiology" where demonstration and proclamation *both* stand at the forefront.[3]

Some of you are reading about power and healing and you're still feeling like I just don't get your scenario. You're still pushing against this idea because of the specific nature of your pain. I invite you to reflect for a moment and consider whether you might be looking for resources instead of rescue. I know we can't all sit down so I can hear each of your stories. But what if that instinct that says no one understands is a search for the resource of empathy rather than the rescue of a Savior? What if you're showing up to a faith community looking for a friend? Or trying to make your circumstances easier? Or pursuing a quick fix to your marriage or a safeguard for your kids' morality?

The weakness with this is clear. While these are all good and necessary things, *they aren't the main thing.* They just aren't. And this story tells us why. The truth about Jesus' power in our lives is simple and worthy of a survival tip:

An Extra Bit of Ordinary

There is one more piece to this story. It's probably my favorite part. It has nothing to do with the defense Peter and John gave (we'll come to that in later chapters). Rather, this is all about the response of those accusers.

"WHEN THEY SAW THE COURAGE OF PETER AND JOHN AND REALIZED THAT THEY WERE UNSCHOOLED, ORDINARY MEN, THEY WERE ASTONISHED AND TOOK NOTE THAT THESE MEN HAD BEEN WITH JESUS."

(ACTS 4:13)

I hope you highlight and underline those words as boldly as you can in this book. This story doesn't say the accusers were amazed because these men were known to have been with the first church of Jesus, or that they were a part of the only true denomination. The response doesn't put—not even for an instant—their relationship with their faith community first. Instead, all over this response is a clear picture of the anchor point of their faith web—Peter and John spent time with Jesus. And that made the difference.

Remember: Your affections must be rightly ordered. Jesus first, everything else second. Always.

[1] Guthrie, Stan. The Other Side of Church Growth: Interview with Philip Jenkins. *Christianity Today.* 18 Mar, 2009.

[2] Olson, David T. *The American Church in Crisis.* Grand Rapids, Zondervan. 2008.

[3] Stetzer, Ed. "You Don't Accidentally Evangelize: If You Don't Prioritize It, It Won't Happen." *Christianity Today*. 22 Jul. 2009.

Three

Well-Dressed People Getting Really Pissed Off

I'd love it if we were having each of these conversations over coffee. Well, in this chapter I'd love it if we could take a field trip. I'd like to take you back to my elementary school and walk with you down the halls and out the door of one of the classrooms that connected directly to our asphalt playground. We'd walk toward one back corner of the blacktop where there might still be a square drawn out of paint. This square would have a cross painted in the middle of it, dividing the larger square into four smaller squares, creating one of the most epic games ever known to 2nd through 5th grade boys—Foursquare.

Foursquare games embody about 95% of my elementary recess memories. I remember this game because it was a blacktop game, which meant that even if it was raining my friends and I could still play. It was an every day outside game, and we took it very, very seriously.

Foursquare—the game of choice on our grade school playground. Now, if you don't know foursquare, there are a few rules you need to understand. Four players inhabited the four squares numbered 1 through 4. Number 1 was the server, and number 4 was the lowest on the totem pole. Number 1 would serve the ball to another player and it had to land inside the squares with a bounce.

At this point, whichever player inhabited the square that had been served to was then tasked with tapping the ball on to another square, with another bounce. This continued until someone misplayed the ball by hitting it out, missing a tap, letting it double bounce, or whatever move might compromise their play. If this happened, the player was eliminated from their square and players moved up the ladder of numbers. So, if number 1 was out, number 2 would move to 1 and become the server, and so on. The line of players outside the square would then see the next person move to square 4 and the game would continue, an endless cycle of elimination and victory.

Two other important rules. First, no spikes; in other words, you couldn't slam the ball down with the force of a cannon. And second, the line was in, not out. Now, I don't know if those were the same rules for your foursquare games, but those were ours—clear and simple. But here's the crazy thing.

When I think of recess games like foursquare, I recall two things. First, I remember incredible amounts of fun. If someone invited me to a foursquare tournament today, I would suit up without hesitation (by suiting up I mean shorts and tennis shoes). Second, in addition to the fun, I also remember an incredible amount of arguing. Like, I can't separate the fun from the fighting in those games.

When the Church Feels Like Recess Gone Bad

Here's a very real question: Why is it that so many of our churches today end up feeling like the recess arguments of our playground days? There's fun, for sure, but it's almost impossible to separate the fun from the fighting. My guess is if you've been in a faith community for any length of time you understand what I'm saying. It's incredibly common for the church to end up feeling just like a bad version of your elementary foursquare games.

One of the core tenets I hold in this book is that the people I know today who don't like the church have little to no problem with Jesus. While they have no problems with Jesus, the thought of Christians? Yeah, that turns their stomachs. So, when we start to talk about the ingrown, ongoing argumentation that often defines our churches, we are pressing into one of the primary reasons why so many people have walked away from the wonky church.

Fist Fighting at the Middle School Youth Group

Once upon a time, I was employed as one of two youth pastors at a very large church in Pittsburgh. My primary focus was 7-8th grade students, and I loved it. Every week we would create a night of controlled chaos with crazy games, fun music, and some stories and teaching that invited these students to learn how to follow Jesus. I used to joke that in ministry with middle schoolers, you worked for 2-3 years of their middle school existence for 30 seconds of meaningful interaction. It was hard, but when they got something spiritual, they really got it.

One night of our midweek program, I watched the crowd while the band played and out of the corner of my eye I saw an instant commotion. I turned to get a better view and saw two of our little seventh grade boys trying desperately to figure out how to have a fist fight with each other. They weren't very good at it, but they were trying, and they were *really* angry.

As always happens in a middle school fight, the crowd formed a ceremonial circle to observe this train wreck while the band played on. I hustled over, grabbed the boys, and told them I wanted to see them in my office (while trying to suppress my own laughter at watching their awkwardness). When we reached the office I gave an inspired lecture complete with guilt trips explaining how ridiculous it was that two of our core-committed middle schoolers could be fighting when we had first-time guests and how could they get in a fight at *youth group* and what might that say to anyone who didn't even know what Jesus' people were like!? It was an epic lecture.

And you know what these two middle schoolers did? They started laughing and agreed with me. Then they shook hands (as awkwardly as they tried to fight with each other), walked out of my office together, and headed back into the worship time. Just like that. Amazing, huh? Sounds like what Jesus' people are supposed to be.

Vagrant Christians and "the Dones"

I will never forget the family who began attending a church where I served on staff. They were the kind of family you're really excited to see in your church— full of life, interested in serving, highly engaged, and ready to worship. I offered to grab coffee with the husband and talk a bit about what some next steps might be as they connected with our faith community.

"Grabbing coffee" turned out to be an hour and a half that morning listening to this man complain about his egotistical pastor, their past church's manipulative ministry teams, and all the horrible people who had let them down at the church they'd just left. We never talked about our church at all.He simply vented about his previous church and all the hurt and anger his family (i.e. he and his wife) still carried from that experience.

Now, I am a pastor – shepherd, as we discussed earlier – and counseling is a part of that role. Because of that, I fully understand the need people have to vent, to process, to share so that there can be healing. In fact, I believe that's part of what the book of James teaches.

"THEREFORE, CONFESS YOUR SINS TO EACH OTHER AND PRAY FOR
EACH OTHER SO THAT YOU MAY BE HEALED."
(JAMES 5:16)

We need to get things out – the things we've committed and the things we've had committed against us. I'm okay with that.

But in the case of this man, his anger never subsided. We met several times for breakfast and every conversation was the same—more griping, more gossip, more criticism of his past congregation/leaders, and more anger. There was never any movement past the anger. So, it wasn't a surprise to me a few months later when his family took offense with the fact that due to my own schedule constraints, I couldn't attend his daughter's baptism, and they decided to leave our church as well. Yes, they joined another church in town. It also didn't surprise me that I began hearing from others in our small-town about how mad this guy was at me. The only thing that has surprised me in all this is that he's been in this current church for over a couple years and seems, well, happy.

I mean no disrespect to this man and his family, but they stand for me as one type of folks that enter our churches so often: the Vagrant Christians. You might also know them as the Angry Christians. Regardless, these are the ones who have either been hurt and become angry, or caused hurt and become angry, and decided to migrate their worship involvement to another congregation in hopes that their menu of problems and issues will disappear. But they're usually surprised to find that their issues follow them wherever they go. When there's no forgiveness, the fist-fighting is just going to break out in another congregation somewhere down the road.

If the Vagrant Christians are migrating from church to church, carrying their anger with them, there's another group that have simply surrendered their anger and found an easier way of life outside their religious setting. They have forsaken the trouble of dealing with the wonkiness of church and simply found a new way of faith outside the traditional congregation. These are the ones who were looking for a fun game with the foursquare ball and when they saw all the arguing they took their own ball and went home. These are people who Joshua Packard describes as "The Dones."

"The Dones" are people who are disillusioned with church. Though they were committed to the church for years—often as lay leaders—they no longer attend. Whether because they're dissatisfied with the structure, social message, or politics of the institutional church, they've decided they are better off without organized religion. As one of our respondents put it, 'I guess the church just sort of churched the church out of me.'"[1]

Conflict: I Do Not Think This Means What You Think it Means

Do you remember Inigo Montoya in the classic film *The Princess Bride*? He has all the great one-liners, but my favorite is: "You keep using this word. I do not think it means what you think it means." One of the problems in our churches is that we misunderstand what we mean when we say "conflict," and because of that we misdirect our attention. If you look up a definition of it in the dictionary, you'll find something along the lines of "disagreement about values, goals, methods, or the facts of a given situation." While this may be a textbook definition, when it comes to conflict today, it is not what most people mean. What they actually mean is more along the lines of this: *"I feel bad. Someone is making me feel bad. I don't like these feelings."*

This may sound like common sense, but it needs to be named. The conflict we experience in our churches doesn't have as much to do with theological struggles, intellectual dissonance, or even leadership failures as it does our emotions of hurt, anger, fear, shame, and regret. As I said, naming this opens the door for not only the hard work of forgiveness but also the harder work of vulnerability and surrender, which are the only meaningful doorways to true reconciliation, and to moving forward in love.

Back to Corinth: The "OG" Religious Playground

The early churches in Acts and Corinth were anything but idealistic notions of what the Church should be. In fact, you might say they were downright jacked-up. Paul knew about playground brawls, and he experienced his own versions of Gypsy Christians and the Dones. He understood the things that caused conflict and he was courageous enough to engage these issues with a healthy mix of grace and truth.

In chapter 5 of his first letter to the Corinthians, Paul follows his opening dialogue about the true nature of leadership in the church by diving headfirst into what had to be a sticky and awkward situation at work in this early body of believers:

"IT IS ACTUALLY REPORTED THAT THERE IS SEXUAL IMMORALITY AMONG YOU, AND OF A KIND THAT EVEN PAGANS DO NOT TOLERATE: A MAN IS SLEEPING WITH HIS FATHER'S WIFE. AND YOU ARE PROUD!"
(1 COR. 5:1-2A)

It was the secret in the church that everybody knew but nobody was talking about. Martin had a torrid night with his stepmom. The word got out, and they all showed up to worship the next week as if all was okay. Paul says some were making jokes about this, boasting about how the whole thing was just so funny. Except it wasn't.

Corinth doesn't feel too far from our own Sunday settings, does it? My hunch is most of you wouldn't have to think too long to come up with a situation where what happened on Saturday night was being whispered and giggled about on Sunday morning. My further hunch is you knew about it and they knew about it and the pastor knew about it, and just like Corinth, no one dealt with it.

> *"SHOULDN'T YOU RATHER HAVE GONE INTO MOURNING AND HAVE PUT OUT OF YOUR FELLOWSHIP THE MAN WHO HAS BEEN DOING THIS?"*
>
> *(1 COR. 5:2B)*

Paul takes the gloves off, telling the church they should

> *"HAND THIS MAN OVER TO SATAN FOR THE DESTRUCTION OF THE FLESH, SO THAT HIS SPIRIT MAY BE SAVED ON THE DAY OF THE LORD"*
>
> *(1 COR. 5:5)*

Now, let me just say this is not a sermon I've ever preached. Nor is it a sermon I would be excited to preach. But it's exactly the sermon Paul preached. And it's exactly the sermon the Corinthians needed. And it may be exactly the sermon our churches today need, as unpopular as it is.

Grace, Grace, Grace (and Truth?)

I started dreaming about the possibility of planting a church way back in 2002. For an entire decade I had countless conversations with my journal, my wife, and my friends about what it would mean to create a congregational community that would truly welcome people just as they were.

In nearly all of those conversations the tribe around me had a sense that for too long the church as we knew it had put too many fence posts and rails around the path to finding Jesus. We knew lost people who couldn't bypass the religious legalism they had been shown in order to find the grace of Christ. For all of those years, as we talked of starting a new community of faith, we dreamed of a place where grace was celebrated. And I still feel that way.

Eight and half years into church planting, I still believe people need to know the grace of Jesus as the transformative catalyst in their lives. I believe the power of grace that unleashed an adulterer with reckless mercy still collides with the lives of those who need an encounter with the Savior today. I am, more now than ever before, committed to seeing the love of Christ poured out on those who think they are unlovable.

With that said, I believe there is another conversation I bypassed during that decade. It is the prophetic conversation. It is the conversation God's people need to have with each other. It is the conversation Paul had the courage to call out in this awkward sermon he sent to the Corinthian carousers boasting of their wild Saturday night with stepmom that permeates our own congregations in so many different expressions today. It is the conversation of Truth when our churches are filled with hypocrisy.

WONKY CHURCH SURVIVAL TIP #6:
COMMITTING TO THE CHURCH CARRIES WITH IT THE RE-
SPONSIBILITY TO PROTECT THE INTEGRITY OF GOD'S
PRESENCE AMONG HIS PEOPLE.

Unpopular Opinions and Hard Conversations

This is one of the most difficult tips I'm going to offer in *Wonky*. But it is crucial for the Me's in the church to become a unified We. This is one of those things the Church—and all of us who continue to love and seek the best for the Church—must commit to. And it is one of the most counter-cultural ways of life we will share together.

It is not common today to speak truth to each other unless that truth is about the good we see in each other. We love hearing encouraging words. We love being told how powerful we are. We are celebrated on social media and rarely held accountable. We are surrounded with "our people" who speak to us consistently of how amazing, beautiful, creative, fun, and strong we are. We instantaneously receive prayers and "good vibes" any time we need them. But we rarely find ourselves with those who look us deeply in the eyes and find the courage to say, "I love you, but you're wrong." Or, "I am committed to standing with you no matter what, but you're being a jerk in your sinfulness right now."

But you know what? When we find ourselves walking beside others we call brothers and sisters in Christ, these are the conversations that should be common among us. These are the conversations that protect the integrity of God's presence among His people. Paul's frustration with the man sleeping with his stepmom has nothing to do with Paul attacking a weaker brother. But it has everything to do with understanding that the congregation is the representation of Christ's Body on earth (1 Cor. 12:27), the Holy Temple of God (2 Cor. 3:16), and the very Bride of Christ (Ephesians 5:21-33). These are far more than metaphors. They signify holy spaces never to be spat upon, defiled, or degraded through religious hypocrisy that repeats itself simply because the people of God are unwilling to have hard conversations.

Paul echoes a problem the Church still faces today—an unwillingness to deal with sin that manifests itself in our committed brothers and sisters. What is so fascinating about this is that today the Church has gotten better at calling out the sins of unbelievers who don't follow Jesus than we have calling out the sins of each other. Look around. It won't take long for you to track down some religious setting on social media, your newsfeed, or even in the side conversations of your local congregation where the religious superiors (the ones doing the talking) are tearing apart the sins of others who don't even belong to their fellowship (and by the way, never will). Paul keeps punching.

"I WROTE TO YOU IN MY LETTER NOT TO ASSOCIATE WITH SEXUALLY IMMORAL PEOPLE—NOT AT ALL MEANING THE PEOPLE OF THIS WORLD WHO ARE IMMORAL, OR THE GREEDY AND SWINDLERS, OR IDOLATERS. IN THAT CASE YOU WOULD HAVE TO LEAVE THIS WORLD. BUT NOW I AM WRITING TO YOU THAT YOU MUST NOT ASSOCIATE WITH ANYONE WHO CLAIMS TO BE A BROTHER OR SISTER BUT IS SEXUALLY IMMORAL OR GREEDY, AN IDOLATER OR SLANDERER, A DRUNKARD OR SWINDLER. DO NOT EVEN EAT WITH SUCH PEOPLE"
(1 COR. 5:9-12)

Don't miss this. Paul isn't speaking of unbelievers here. He isn't interested in challenging the morality of those who don't believe in Jesus. In fact, Paul would seem to suggest that it's ridiculous for believers to expect non-believers to have any moral framework when they don't follow Jesus (1 Cor. 5:12-13). Wow, wouldn't this change our broader cultural conversations if we really embraced this? Paul says, I'm talking about *you!* *You* believers. *You* Christians. *You* church-people who claim to follow Jesus.

All too often today we are condoning the sins of our community while condemning the sins of the crowd.

Paul calls out the disgust of this awkward incident in the Corinthian church (and don't think for a moment this wasn't awkward!) because he is more committed to the integrity of the worship and honor given to God among this body of believers than he is to their own comfort with each other. Paul is acting on this by actually trusting the prayer Jesus prayed for all believers:

> *"...FOR THOSE WHO WILL BELIEVE IN ME THROUGH THEIR [ALL BELIEVERS'] MESSAGE, THAT ALL OF THEM MAY BE ONE, FATHER, JUST AS YOU ARE IN ME AND I AM IN YOU. MAY THEY ALSO BE IN US SO THAT THE WORLD MAY BELIEVE THAT YOU HAVE SENT ME"*
> *(JOHN 17:20-21)*

Notice that simple phrase "so that." Jesus prays for unity in his church *so that* the world may believe. Jesus seems to believe—and he was God, so he probably understood theology fairly well—that when the Church functions in unity the result will be an undeniable demonstration of the power and presence of God in the body of believers. Because of this, Paul says we have to stop putting up with believers who aren't living like believers.

Now, I know this is a fine line. I know it sounds like I'm promoting something that could actually perpetuate greater disharmony, in-fighting, back-biting, and a culture of judgment passed on each other at the drop of a hat. Perhaps this line of thinking plays right into our current cancel culture. I also know what I'm about to say sounds overly idealistic; but, I think we assume that to be the natural result because once again, we are putting the church ahead of Jesus on our priority list. When we hear claims that we should regularly hold each other accountable, speak truth to each other as believers, and work for integrity in the body of believers, we automatically think about how uncomfortable we will be, or how uncomfortable the other person will be in that process. What we don't think about naturally is what Paul was consumed with in this passage. That's right—purity.

Giving Up the Right to be Right

As I'm writing this chapter, there's a bit of my own story I've been avoiding. A couple years ago I walked through one of the most painful seasons of ministry I've ever experienced. A great friend, and someone who had partnered with us in the journey of church planting from the very beginning began to distance themselves from me. Not from our church, from me. It was one of those spaces where you know the relationship isn't well, but you're not really sure how to fix it. Let me be completely candid here--I fully believe I carry a good deal of the weight in this relational breakdown. Looking at the decline of this relationship, I see many points where I should have entered the conflict and approached the issues at hand with more intentionality and greater compassion. In that season, in many ways, I became the failed pastor I described in the first chapter.

With that said, the most painful moment of this entire journey for me was when this friend uttered the simple statement: "This is beyond repair." This came after more than a season of awkwardness. It came after withdrawal, relational distancing, a refusal to attend worship and "sit under my leadership" while still choosing to serve as a leader in a key ministry area of our faith community. It came after false statements were made and meetings without my knowledge were held. It came with a great deal of toxicity and an unveiling of this individual's broken past and hurt at the hands of her own trauma. And it came with the refusal to pursue healing. "This is beyond repair."

This broken relationship ended the opportunity for love. It triangulated others into the hurt in ways where the damage is still felt. It created a defensive guardedness in me that still leaves me trying to navigate my own issues of trust. It left more than a mark, it left a gaping wound. Again, I carry some responsibility *and* I have been hurt deeply. Both of those pieces can coexist.

Since that moment, this friend has left our congregation. The conflict we experienced found closure, but at what cost? We have, in many ways, taken our four-square balls and said, "Game's over, we're going home." I'm baffled by this because I just fundamentally don't believe a relationship among God's people is ever irreparable. I believe toxic relationships should be closed; abusive relationships should end. But two siblings in Christ, sitting across from each other claiming love for God, should never end the game of grace the Kingdom of God invites them into. Yet, I'm right in the thick of this.

As I've processed this finality, I've recognized something that shifted in me when this friend uttered those words. Hearing those words, something shook loose in my mental capacity and shifted how I engaged our conversation. I stopped trying to be right. In those uttered words, I didn't care that this friend understands me anymore; I didn't want to defend myself; I just wanted to see restoration. I wanted to see a hope for restoration.

One of the major spots I failed in this relationship was a below the surface desire to be right, to be on the higher ground, to be morally superior. I wanted restoration, but I also wanted to be proven just. So often, this is the driving force that perpetuates so much conflict in our churches. While the conflict starts with what I mentioned earlier ("I don't like how someone is making me feel"), it continues because we can't stop thinking, "I want them to know I'm right."

It's fascinating to me that Paul recognizes this same principle at work in the Corinthian church. After his calling out of the sin in chapter 5, he addresses the broader body of believers in chapter 6:

"THE VERY FACT THAT YOU HAVE LAWSUITS AMONG YOU MEANS YOU HAVE BEEN COMPLETELY DEFEATED ALREADY. WHY NOT RATHER BE WRONGED?
WHY NOT RATHER BE CHEATED?"
(1 COR. 6:7)

WONKY CHURCH SURVIVAL TIP #7:
FOR UNITY TO EXIST, WE MUST RELINQUISH THE RIGHT
TO BE RIGHT.

I know this is hard. I'm living it right now. As this relationship ends, I fight the urge to keep trying to explain myself, to triangle others in the conversation and explain what happened, to defend my positions. But the reality is, if the relationship is over, we've both lost. In this moment, in the season where the body of Christ has suffered from conflict, I have no right to be right any longer. And just as Jesus did, I am called to pick up my cross and stay surrendered for the sake of the body.

Jesus Played Four-Square with a Bunch of Cheaters

Did you ever think about how hard this was for Jesus? Not just picking up the cross – which the Scriptures seem to portray as the one thing he couldn't do... He actually needed help carrying his cross. Of course that was excruciating. His suffering was Hell on earth. I'm talking about the difficulty of something else Jesus experienced as he was arrested, beaten, tortured, and killed. Throughout those grueling hours, Jesus experienced several moments where his closest friends completely abandoned him. Judas. Peter. James. Matthew. All of them left him to suffer alone. I cannot imagine the emotional pain this caused in the midst of his physical suffering. I find comfort that Jesus was betrayed more than I ever will be as a pastor.

But you know what's even harder to fathom?

Jesus was fully God. Jesus was also fully human. Throughout the gospels we see the integration of his humanity and divinity revealed in miracles and mud, in inspired teaching and good food around messy tables. With his humanity and divinity in mind, we must realize that Jesus spent three years of intentional ministry prior to his crucifixion knowing that his closest friends, his disciples, his chosen leaders would all fail him. They would let him down. They would leave him when he needed them most. And he chose to put up with it. To endure it. To suffer through it.

> "IN YOUR RELATIONSHIP WITH ONE ANOTHER, HAVE THE SAME MINDSET AS CHRIST JESUS: WHO, BEING IN VERY NATURE GOD, DID NOT CONSIDER EQUALITY WITH GOD SOMETHING TO BE USED TO HIS OWN ADVANTAGE; RATHER, HE MADE HIMSELF NOTHING BY TAKING THE VERY NATURE OF A SERVANT, BEING MADE IN HUMAN LIKENESS. AND BEING FOUND IN APPEARANCE AS A MAN, HE HUMBLED HIMSELF BY BECOMING OBEDIENT TO DEATH—EVEN DEATH ON A CROSS!"
> (PHP. 2:5-8)

For those of you willing to reimagine the Church with me, this is what we are called to. We are called to forgive. We are called to unity.

We are called to die to self even when we know we're right. We are called to be obedient to death, even death for the sake of unity. We are called to have a Jesus mindset, and that makes all the difference. That means everything.

[1] Packard, Joshua. "Meet the Dones." https://www.christianityto-day.com/pastors/2015/summer-2015/meet-dones.html.

Four

No One Wants to Read this Chapter

Okay, let's start a difficult chapter with a goofy illustration. Let's say you and your spouse, or maybe a best friend, are going to spend a Friday evening with my wife and me. The plan is to get dressed up and go out to eat together. As we're nailing down details, I shoot you a text and ask, "Where do you want to eat?" Most of us have this politeness about us. We have this thing that is actually scripted in us. If the four of us were going to dinner and I asked where you wanted to eat, I would bet good money that your simple response would be, "I don't care. You pick."

Here's the thing. Let's say you tell me you don't care and I respond with the following: "Awesome. I was thinking about Taco Bell!" Now what happens? It's Friday night. We planned this way in advance. You got dressed up. And we're heading to Taco Bell? Suddenly, you care.

Why Should We Care?

During the run-up to the recent Presidential election, I watched the Vice-Presidential debate. As it concluded, the moderator shared a question from an 8th grade student in Utah. She said it this way: "When I watch the news, all I see is arguing between Democrats and Republicans. When I watch the news, all I see is citizen fighting against citizen. When I watch the news, all I see is two candidates from opposing parties trying to tear each other down. If our leaders can't get along, how are our citizens supposed to get along? Your examples could make all the difference to bring us together."

If you don't get anything else out of this chapter (I hope you do though), maybe that question from one of our children is sufficient to make you pause and consider just what it is we're doing in the political realm and how, like it or not, that has bled over into the Body of Christ. Yes, we're going to talk about politics in this chapter. And here we go.

Realities and Reality

Two realities strike me. First, some of you reading this don't want to talk about politics at all. You're sick of it. It surrounds us. It never gets better. And the supposed leaders of our country seem to have nothing but their own best interests at heart. I feel you. As I'm writing, it's 2020 and we have just come through (or are still coming through) one of the ugliest elections we've ever seen. Political fatigue is real.

Second, some of you obsess about politics. In fact, you hold your perspective tightly, as one of the centerpieces of what you assume it means to express your faith. For the conservatives, to be Christian means to be pro-life, and you cannot fathom any worldview centered on Jesus that doesn't vote for those who are pro-life. For the progressives, God's heart beats for the immigrant, and to pursue a political candidate who would close our borders seems counter to the Gospel.

So, with those realities in mind, I know the reality is that I lose in this chapter by talking about politics and the Church. If you need to skip ahead to the next chapter, you have my blessing. But, if the conversation matters—if the strange intertwining of politics and faith that's been around as long as God's people have been around—if that matters in a way that you believe, as I do, that it must be acknowledged and discussed and reimagined, then read on. Struggle against my thoughts. Wrestle with your own beliefs. But by all means consider this. The relationship between the church and politics - or even the church and the broader culture - has always been, and will always be, filled with incredible complexity.

It Ain't Easy

> WONKY CHURCH SURVIVAL TIP #8:
>
> DON'T EVER EXPECT THE INTERSECTION OF THE
> CHURCH AND POLITICS TO BE EASY.

Politics isn't easy, and it shouldn't be. And when you weave that into the way of Christ-followers, called to intersect with our broader political landscape, it becomes even more difficult. It is complex, multi-layered, and should cause us to wrestle. When you study Scriptures about the way the people of Jesus should engage the culture you discover a list of principles that seems to portray several political approaches:

"Do not be conformed to the pattern of this world, but be transformed..." Rom. 12:2

"Do not love the world or the things in the world..." 1 John 2:15

"Therefore go out from their midst, and be separate from them..." 2 Cor. 6:17

Daniel stood as a high authority in the Babylonian royalty and their political machine.

Joseph – the rescuer of Israel during the famine – only did so by working within the Egyptian palace. (Genesis 39)

King David was sanctioned as King "after God's own heart" in spite of his many, many flaws. (1 and 2 Samuel)

Each of these verses and illustrations paints a very complex relationship between the movement of God through individuals/people and the political realm of the day. The passages from Romans, 1 John, and 2 Corinthians all seem to demand that the followers of Christ resist the temptation to look like, think like, act like, or become like the dominant culture of the day, even at times suggesting a separation as necessary. And yet, we see in the stories of Daniel, Joseph, and even King David where the political world of the day seems to be the very place where God would have his people not just wade in but dive head first as a part of their calling. So, what role should Christians - and the Church – have in politics?

The Menu: Christ and Culture

During a recent bucket-list type trip to Ireland with my family, it felt like we were never more than fifty meters from a pub. It sorta felt like churches on street corners in the South. But in each of these pubs, the menus were almost always the same: soup, French fries (chips), some sort of seafood, and an assortment of main dishes that included some types of meat, sandwiches, and more. And as you might guess, every pub served beer, lots and lots of beer, especially Guinness. The longer we were in Ireland the easier it was to order food, because we knew what was on the menu.

The question of how Christians should engage politics—and the broader culture—is no new question. In fact, from the first days of the Church, the followers of Jesus have struggled to figure out what it means to be faithful to Christ and a force in the broader world. Taxes, issues of morality, calls to revolution, party lines—these are not new areas of engagement for the people of Christ. But many of us find ourselves confused and reactionary to the political conversations around us because of one main reason: we don't understand the menu.

Back in 1951, a German theologian named Richard Niebuhr wrote an important little book dealing directly with the question of Christians and culture. For a long time, Niebuhr's five views of Christ and culture have served as the menu for followers of Jesus. He provides, in many ways, the various options for those who wish to engage the broader world with faithfulness to Christ. I'll briefly describe these options, along with some examples and the difficulties of each view.

Christ AGAINST Culture. This view rejects any assumption that the broader culture, and for our thoughts the political systems of a culture, deserves a Christian's allegiance. The belief here is that what is sinful has always come directly from the culture; and therefore, Christians should separate themselves (sometimes literally as with the Amish and Mennonite communities) from the broader world. The tension point for this view is that it is impossible to fully achieve this separation. Even the most loyal of the Christ AGAINST culture folks cannot separate entirely. Not to mention, this view tends to miss the reality that God himself, in the act of Creation, established culture and systems that were very, very good. Ultimately, the Christ against culture view takes a protective stance, albeit with good intentions but difficult efforts.

Christ OF Culture. Niebuhr's second view lies on the opposite end of the spectrum and sees no great tension between the Church and the broader world, nor the social laws and the Gospel. Those who hold this view interpret culture *through* Christ himself (thus seeing a lens for interpreting the best laws, ethics, and political perspectives). Often represented in the movements of liberal Protestantism, these adherents find a positive relationship with the broader world on behalf of Christ. But the danger is that the views toward good morality can serve to water down the more difficult teaching and claims of Jesus himself. What this leads to is assimilation rather than transformation.

Christ ABOVE culture. A more moderate option, this view sees no battle between Christ and culture, but rather the tension lying between God and humanity. God creates and orders humanity; so, it is neither good nor bad. When humanity sins, rebellion is expressed in cultural terms. Moral law and Christian involvement in society is possible and the Church carries its spiritual purpose into its earthly existence. This moderate view can be seen in Roman Catholicism, as well as others who see Christians living in both realms and trying to assert Christ's dominance over culture. The danger here is that Christ and Gospel can be institutionalized and the softness of its effect on the larger world can be missed.

Christ IN PARADOX with culture. Adherents here wish to hold to a loyalty to Christ and a responsibility for culture, but they perceive this through a lens that considers the brokenness of culture as something to be repaired. While this view (held traditionally by many denominational traditions including Lutheranism) does capture the tension of Christians in the world today, it can grow somewhat stagnant in answering the questions of a Jesus follower's relationship to the more pressing and urgent issues faced today.

Christ the TRANSFORMER OF culture. Finally, Niebuhr conceives of conversionists who hold a hopeful view of culture. This perspective assumes God as Creator—thus, culture is good and therefore can be transformed and given to the glory of God. It is the responsibility of Jesus' people then to work for the good of culture, which includes—wait for it—politics.

(Take a deep breath in. Now let it out)

Yes, that's some heavy philosophical ground we just covered. And before we come back to the lighter ground let me ask which of these five feels most familiar to you? What does your religious background tell you about the perspectives held in your tradition? Whatever tradition you emerged from, it's safe to say that none of us grew up completely removed from these conversations. We all had some sort of menu to choose from.

Church Ostriches - Why We Need to Get Political

So, back to some real-life application. In the early 19th century, there is case after case of churches that resisted speaking out against slavery because that was what we would now call, "getting too political." We hear this even today, right? "Don't get too political. Just preach the Gospel." I taught a series leading up to the most recent political election about being citizens of the Kingdom and literally had folks stop coming for those four weeks and immediately returned once it was over. *Church Ostriches* – heads go down in the sand when it gets too uncomfortable. The problem with this posture is that those churches of the early 19th century were complicit in the sin of slavery even as they just "preached the gospel." Yeah, what about us?

In their excellent book *Winsome Persuasion: Christian Influence in a Post-Christian World*, Tim Muehlhoff and Richard Langer reference a number of "scripts" that many of us live with today. One of them, in regard to the political realm, is what they call it the Argument Script.[1] It is our prescribed way of discussing politics—especially online—with those who hold different views. The way this script works is simple: When we engage with someone who holds a different political opinion, we automatically move toward an "adversarial frame of mind." We argue with this person, or these people, who are now enemies. Why? Simply because we disagree. Here are a few characteristics of the Argument Script that will sound and feel familiar.

First of all, *consideration equals condoning*. If you even consider someone else's perspective, you are compromising. Your preferred political tribe will identify you as a traitor. For example, let's say you are a Republican but you're engaging someone who is pro-choice and rather than simply telling them why they are wrong you look to understand why they think the way they do. Chances are, in today's climate, your tribe (in this case, your Republican friends) will consider you weak. And let's be honest here, this is often an incredibly strong view within the Church community because we are so afraid of our beliefs (political or theological) falling apart.

Second, *monologue above dialogue*. If you dialogue with the opposition, not only are your beliefs going to be on rocky soil, you are conceding an argument you know you can win. Monologues (what these authors call calculated monologues) cause us to draw conclusions well in advance of the conversation. Full of assumptions, we respond in our head before we've ever heard what the other side is trying to communicate.

Third, in the Argument Script, disagreeing is not enough. *Demonization is the way forward*. The common approach today is one political group identifies their beliefs as sacred, and in order to defend their beliefs they use language in such a way that the opposing viewpoint is seen as evil. Need some examples? *All Democrats want to kill babies. All Republicans hate immigrants. Every Democrat is a socialist. Every Republican is racist. If you're feminist, you hate men. If you're Christian, you are intolerant and hateful.* Sounds and feels familiar, doesn't it?

Finally, Muelhoff and Langer discuss our specifically online Argument Scripts as being filled with *disinhibition*. This is so important. Communication experts see disinhibition as the way we feel unrestrained by the normal social conventions that occur when we are face to face, in person. In the online realm, our disagreements happen through communication without filters. We say things to the people we disagree with that we would never say were we face to face. Why? Because in the online, *disinhibited* world we cannot see the anger or hurt our words cause, and so we have no ability and no need to empathize. We are removed from our rival, and they are removed from us.

This is our script. We have all been victims and we have all been perpetrators of this script. And frankly, it's not working. Especially in the Church. I have friends leaving Jesus because the people of faith are enamored with this Argument Script. We demonize before we empathize. We idolize before we analyze. And for all our political arguments, I believe the Wonky Church has lost sight of the great value God places on hearts above issues. So, in the remainder of this chapter I want to consider how Paul approached one of the key arguments of his day in the city of Corinth.

A Restaurant Debate

In 1 Corinthians 8, Paul leaves the conversation of marriage and shifts to where people in the church were going to eat their meals. No kidding. He moves from sex and marriage to, well, restaurants. But the restaurants of Paul's day were a bit different than ours.

N.T. Wright describes such a restaurant as an ancient temple.[2] This temple, in the first century, would have been a place given to the worship of false gods and the Roman emperors. In these temples, citizens of the empire would come with animals for sacrifice, and after the sacrifice had been made the remains would be cooked and the family would have a meal right there in the temple. When this involved larger sacrifices, a good deal of meat was left over and the remains might be sold to other temple attendees just as restaurants today serve their own food. So, as Paul begins this chapter, he is confronting a very serious argument taking place in the early Church: "Should believers in Jesus eat food that had been sacrificed to idols?"

> *"NOW ABOUT FOOD SACRIFICED TO IDOLS: WE KNOW THAT 'WE ALL POSSESS KNOWLEDGE.'"*
>
> *(1 COR. 8:1)*

For just a moment, consider your thoughts and feelings when you hear the following statements:

* * *

Make America Great Again!

(President Donald Trump's 2016 campaign

slogan)

* * *

Yes We Can!

President Barack Obama's 2008 campaign

slogan)

* * *

Just Do It!

(Nike mantra)

* * *

My pleasure.

(Chick-Fil-A employee relationship code)

* * *

My hunch is that you have a great deal of feelings beyond just reading these simple sentences. Prior to 2016, if someone had said,

"Make America great again," we would have probably assumed this was a great sentiment. Now, we have an entire system of politics, agendas, regime, and personalities associated with this phrase. It's the same with Obama's slogan. So much exists beyond the words. Nike has built an entire culture on their mantra. And Chick-Fil-A has developed a fan base almost without equal.

When Paul quotes this familiar statement from the Corinthian culture, "We all possess knowledge," he is depicting more than words, but an entire way of thinking. Basically, there were Jesus followers who believed they "got it" more clearly than others. They had a secret knowledge that allowed them to eat whatever they wanted. And Paul speaks directly to this knowledge:

"BUT KNOWLEDGE PUFFS UP WHILE LOVE BUILDS UP"

(1 COR. 8:1B)

Paul moves forward in this section by calling out the nature of idols and the character of Yahweh. He quotes more of this common "knowledge", stating that, "An idol is nothing at all in this world," and, "There is no God but one" (1 Cor. 8:4). Among the Christians of this time, Paul was stating simple, doctrinal truths. He was keeping things simple. And yet, I think there was a bit more than the statement of facts taking place. I think Paul was calling out the believers who were lost in arguments to the stark reality of their own idolatry.

WONKY CHURCH SURVIVAL TIP #9:
WE HAVE TO COME CLEAN ABOUT OUR IDOLS.

If we're to find a new way forward in our politics, a new way of disagreeing with those around us, a new script built on love, then we have to come clean about our idols. I understand we don't live in Roman cities full of polished temples, but idolatry and the sacrifices demanded by our own idols remain a critical piece of our daily lives—especially in the political realm. We live in a political climate where it's all too easy to be sucked into the culture of charisma coming from our preferred political leader, or the preferred candidate; and it's easy to allow this to carry us to the point of idolatry.

The truth is that ideologies and popular political leaders can consume our attention to the point of idolatrous worship. We live with the reality that most of us would rather talk about idolatry through the lens of first century Roman shrines rather than 21st century American media. Yet, for some of us, we find ourselves worshipping at the shrines of CNN or FoxNews more consistently than at the throne of Jesus. The Word of God, as we believe intellectually, may have authority, but if something comes from our preferred political news source then we will orient our lives and political opinions to the views of our false gods.

We have to come clean about our idols because our idols are unashamed of trying to gain our worship. While we may believe there is only one God, we rally and argue for our candidates or our party's positions as if their divinity is higher than Yahweh's. Daniel Shapiro, the author of *Negotiating the Nonnegotiable*, says it this way: "There is an allure to this kind of politics, a sense of falling, of vertigo. We fall in love with a candidate. We fall in hatred toward another. We fall through a dizzying, contagious mixture of appeals to loyalty and identity."[3] My friends, this is a textbook definition of idolatry.

The Worthlessness of Food

"BUT FOOD DOES NOT BRING US NEAR TO GOD; WE ARE NO WORSE
IF WE DO NOT EAT,
AND NO BETTER IF WE DO"
(1 COR. 8:8)

Paul seems to be arguing on behalf of those who are okay with eating in the temples. He says food really has no way of drawing us closer to God or not. Again, Paul is keeping this simple. He says, "It doesn't matter. Eat or don't eat. It's up to you."

Slight digression here. As a Christian teenager, I used to think anyone I saw with a beer was really making God mad! I mean, come on, it's alcohol! Are you kidding me? That stuff makes you drunk! Now the older I got, the clearer this became to me. If you're a recovering alcoholic, then of course alcohol isn't a good idea. If you're under 21 years of age, then you're disobeying the law of our land and Scripture is clear on the sinfulness of that. But for those who don't battle alcoholism, and who like me are able to enjoy a good glass of wine or a great craft beer, don't get caught up in thinking this is a spiritual issue. Theologians call these gray areas "Christian liberties"— places where Scripture doesn't read like a checklist. Alcohol has some gray to it. Drunkenness and lack of self-control don't. But in moderation, there is liberty.

Now, back to our politics. Most—*most* political issues fall into the category of Christian liberties. I know this is controversial today, but Jesus is so much bigger than letting himself be co-opted by any one political party. He just is. As one great preacher says, "Jesus didn't come to take sides, he came to take over." Please, let me be clear. I'm not talking about inarguable biblical issues. I'm not saying you can make a political argument that murder is okay. I don't believe you can convince someone biblically that justice doesn't matter.

Those things are uber-clear—not gray. But I am talking about all the other stuff. Questions like this:

- What type of economic system works best?
- How much involvement should the government have in day-to-day life?
- What is the best way to solve immigration?
- How should healthcare work?

The reality is there are vast canyons of freedom here, as there are with so many areas of our faith! And when we realize this, when we embody this, we can finally enter new conversations, new political disagreements, and new discussions that enrich and challenge each other with biblical truth and love and move us deeper in our faith without demonizing someone who brings their own interpretations to the conversations.

Let Love Rule

Wouldn't it be great if Paul ended there? It would be excellent if he told us the food doesn't matter, and we're free to eat where we want. But he doesn't.

> "BE CAREFUL, HOWEVER, THAT THE EXERCISE OF YOUR RIGHTS
> DOES NOT BECOME A STUMBLING BLOCK TO THE WEAK"
> (1 COR. 8:9)

Talk about flipping the script. Just when these Corinthian food-ies think, "Look, Paul agrees with us!," he takes the discussion to a new place:

> "FOR IF SOMEONE WITH A WEAK CONSCIENCE SEES YOU, WITH ALL
> YOUR KNOWLEDGE, EATING IN AN IDOL'S TEMPLE, WON'T THAT PERSON
> BE EMBOLDENED TO EAT WHAT IS SACRIFICED TO IDOLS? SO THIS
> WEAK BROTHER OR SISTER, FOR WHOM CHRIST DIED, IS DESTROYED BY
> YOUR KNOWLEDGE. WHEN YOU SIN AGAINST THEM IN THIS WAY AND
> WOUND THEIR WEAK CONSCIENCE, YOU SIN AGAINST CHRIST"
> (1 COR. 8:10-12)

But the question we have to ask is—"How are they destroyed? How does the practice of my freedom *in* Christ result in sin *against* Christ?" To answer this, we have to go back to the opening of Paul's argument:

> "KNOWLEDGE PUFFS UP BUT LOVE BUILDS UP."
> (1 COR. 8:1)

According to Paul, we destroy others when our arguments—political, cultural, social, emotional, any argument—becomes about our own knowledge of the issue rather than love for the brother or sister we are hurting. We destroy when we're convinced the argument is about us being right rather than them being loved. Paul is summing up a way for the Church to thrive even today. **Our freedom should never destroy the hearts of others.**

If you've been hurt by the wonky nature of the Church and its grotesque intersection with the political landscape of today's personalities and news media, you probably grasp deeply what I'm about to say. And, if you've participated in this gross overlap, you get this too. Because this is where our political positions and perspectives have become the idol that is so deeply ripping our faith communities apart in irreparable ways. Many of the believers I know who follow Jesus and stand as representatives of the Church—including myself—have used our claim to freedom in ways that are destructive. We have become convinced that freedom in Christ is the same as freedom in America. Where freedom in America has equaled an individualistic set of rights, freedom in Christ has always been about love for the other, the weaker, brothers and sisters around us.

WONKY CHURCH SURVIVAL TIP #10:
WE CANNOT BE SO FIXATED ON FREEDOM FOR *ME*
THAT WE FORGET LOVE FOR THE *WE.*

Let me give you some examples of where this happens today in regard to specific political issues. Fair warning—these are hot topic issues.

Abortion. I am pro-life in most cases. And I know women—personally—who have been in the incredibly difficult position of making a choice to have an abortion. And, in those hellish circumstances, and because of the obsession of Christians around them with a political *issue* superseding a personal *crisis*, these women are *still* convinced God hates them.

Homosexuality. I believe the Scriptures teach a consistent theology and ethic that holds up heterosexual marriage and celibacy in singleness as the way of flourishing for men and women. You can disagree with me. Many do. I'm okay with that and I think God is too. But I refuse to believe that a fixation on this issue is worth sacrificing our LGBTQ brothers and sisters to the unbelievable rates of depression and suicide that they face. This hate—whether real or perceived—is a justice issue above all else at this point.

Toxic Masculinity. I believe anyone who abuses or assaults a woman, a child, or a man is committing an egregious sin against the image of God and we—as followers of Jesus—should do everything we possibly can to stop things like this from happening. But I also believe that obsession with this pursuit has been carried so far culturally that we have left a generation of young boys and retired men alike neutered, in a space where their confusion over what it means to be a strong, godly man who follows Jesus is crippling them from living fully into his Kingdom.

What this boils down to is the fact that we have to understand the reality of our own and others' freedom in Christ as being rooted and formed by love for others. Whether it's our Argument Script or the Cancel Culture or whatever the next thing is, anything that shuts any voice down or causes others to walk away from faith, or worse leaves them lost and alienated from the community of faith and any hope of healing—that, my friends, is where the freedom for *me* has caused us to lose sight of love for the *we*.

Paul's Final Argument

> "THEREFORE, IF WHAT I EAT CAUSES MY BROTHER OR SISTER TO FALL INTO SIN, I WILL NEVER EAT MEAT AGAIN, SO THAT I WILL NOT CAUSE THEM TO FALL"
>
> (1 COR. 8:13)

My favorite part of the book *Winsome Persuasion* recounts several cultural moments where prominent political voices found themselves recognizing the great divisions their own Argument Scripts caused. Glenn Beck, the (in)famous conservative commentator, back in 2013, apologized for "any role that I have played in dividing," even as he won a free speech award. After the shooting of U.S. House member Gabby Giffords, and eighteen others in 2011, liberal commentator Keith Olbermann ended his "Worst Person in the World" segment. Sarah Palin removed a portion of her website with the graphic of gun crosshairs over 20 democratic congressional districts. In these realizations, at least for a moment, these men and women seemed to realize the pain and vitriol they had caused.

In Paul's brilliant, love-filled, subversive argument in 1 Corinthians 8, he maintains his call that "Knowledge puffs up, but love builds up," by closing with the argument confronting our own Argument Script.

"…IF WHAT I EAT CAUSES MY BROTHER OR SISTER TO FALL INTO SIN, I WILL NEVER EAT MEAT AGAIN, SO THAT I WILL NOT CAUSE THEM TO FALL"

(1 COR. 8:13)

The answer to the Argument Script, so prevalent today in our political elections, our news media cycles, and our social media wars, is simple: **compassion**. Compassion for our brothers and sisters of every creed, color, and convincing. If we, as followers of Jesus, can model anything as citizens of the Kingdom of God embodying the way of Jesus in our politics, it is the reclamation of compassion and empathy as our primary markers in a world that seems to be losing its mind. Our arguments are not working. It's too easy, too common, too endorsed by political leaders and news pundits today to simply perpetuate the Argument Script. If I'm honest, I really don't care what anyone thinks politically. I care *how* they think it and *how* they present it. And I care, most deeply, about *how we the Church embody the love of Christ* in every realm of life—including our politics.

Remember the 8th grader from Utah's question and challenge: "If our leaders can't get along, how are our citizens supposed to get along? Your examples could make all the difference to bring us together." If we, the followers of Jesus, can't get along, how will the watching world know of the deep, deep love of Jesus? My friends, our example could make all the difference. The world, and our children, are watching.

[1] Muelhoff, Tim and Langer, Richard. *Winsome Persuasion: Christian Influence in a Post-Christian World*. Downers Grove, IVP Academic. 2017.

[2] Wright, N.T. *1 Corinthians: 13 Studies for Individuals and Groups*. Downers Grove, Intervarsity Press. 2009.

[3] Shapiro, Daniel. "Why Are We Addicted to Divisive Politics?" *Time.* 18 Apr. 2016.

Five

Food and Sex

In one of my youth ministry moments that wouldn't make the ESPN highlight reel, a parent asked for a meeting with me. Her daughter, a sweet, homeschooled young lady who was as good-natured as could be, had stopped coming to our program. As I talked with the parents, I found out it was because I had tattoos and the other youth pastor's wife had a nose piercing. In her mother's words (and this is a direct quote), "This youth group is the worldliest place I bring my daughter."

To which I looked at the mother calmly without any filter and without any love and said, "Well... that's not a good thing."

Unkind, I know. True, yes. But my heart was wrong. My spirit was joyful in my quick-wittedness. But my heart was wrong.

What does Worldly Mean?

As we keep exploring the Wonky Church, let me pose this question. Have you ever had the word "worldly" thrown at you? Have you ever had someone talk about how "worldly" something is that you've participated in? Maybe the music you were listening to? Or the show you were watching? The drink you were drinking? Something about material possessions?

When that mother identified our youth group as a worldly place, what she passive-aggressively communicated was that she could not fathom how a youth pastor would have tattoos (even though they were "Jesus-y Hebrew" tattoos) and how the youth pastor's wife thought body piercing her nose was okay. What she really meant by worldly were the things she didn't want her daughter doing, partaking in, practicing, or saying. And to some degree, that's fair.

But here's the wonkiness of this. In every church I've ever served, "worldly" is a spectrum. Every single person has different understandings of worldliness. Some believe R-rated movies to be worldly (at least until Mel Gibson redeemed the R-rating with *The Passion of the Christ*). Yet those same folks keep gossiping in the pews of their church. Some think that any music that doesn't come off the local Christian radio station is worldly music. But some of those same folks couldn't wait for the latest episode of Game of Thrones without ever questioning the content. Others think worldly means—as we talked last chapter—that you're on the wrong side of the political aisle. Some believe alcohol to be the Devil's brew, but their McDonalds addiction may kill them much sooner than my penchant for red wine.

The reality is that all too often we have a concept of worldliness that, like the mother I offended, is self-defined rather than God-defined. And that's just plain wonky. Here's why. That's the very reason some of you have chosen not to follow Jesus, because faith appeared to be nothing but a set of rules: Don't drink. Don't listen to secular music. Don't watch HBO. Don't wear revealing clothing. As the joke used to go— "Don't smoke, don't chew, don't date the girls who do." Except that's not really very funny. Whatever the rules, you were fed a narrative that said if you broke any of the self-defined worldliness standards set up by the prominent voices of your church, God would be upset with you and that was just the tip of the iceberg of consequences.

Some things were okay. But some were not. And if by chance you were in the same church or faith community for a long period of time, then you could sort of figure things out. But if you moved around a little or a lot, you had to figure out the "new" rules at the "new" church. And your question was simple. How can these churches all serve the same Jesus if he keeps changing the rules? **When worldliness is self-defined, there is no consistent standard of how to follow Jesus.** And that's wonky.

Where this leaves us as a broader church culture echoes back several centuries. In nearly every single religion or every philosophical system that exists, there have been some version of these debates. The primary question: what is worldly and what is not? Or you may have experienced it as the secular versus the sacred. And let me reiterate, this is not just a Christian Church debate.

A Tale of Two Tables

Nearly every religious and philosophical system that ever existed has created two tables to show the ends of their worldliness spectrum. First of all, there's the Electric Slide table. If you've ever been to a wedding, when the Electric Slide song comes on, even the atrocious dancers like me find the nerve to get on the floor. On this table, you might put a party hat. Some of those little party favor blowers that make that annoying mouse trumpet noise. This is the table that philosophers, for quite some time, have identified with the label of Hedonism. This table is all about pleasure, and the maximization of pleasure. The goal of life – this worldview – centers on minimizing pain and getting as much "boogie-woogie" (see what I did there?) out of every day as possible. Chase the material things that bring you joy. Don't worry about what is worldly because pleasure is of the highest good. This is the first table.

The second table might be the 9 to 5 table. It might hold a dumb-bell. I say that, because this is the table that takes work and discipline. It is the table philosophers labeled as asceticism. Asceticism comes from the Greek word for "exercise, or training." It is about resistance and discipline, about avoiding any kind of sensual pleasures for the sake of higher spiritual goals or philosophical wisdom. Put in the work to get to the highest good. These two tables set the stage for what we're talking about – the question of worldliness and rules.

Every church I've ever experienced, and every church you've ever experienced, holds some view of what belongs on these tables and what does not. The believers who are a part of the cultures of these churches have assumptions and conclusions (usually self-defined) as to what is okay and what is not. The mom of that sweet girl I mentioned earlier?She considered tattoos and body piercing as a "no-no." Interestingly enough, many Christians today are all about the "yes, yes" table. Everything is okay! There are no limits! Anything goes, man! But is that not just trading one extreme for the other?

Paul Dancing at the Tables

I feel like a broken record at this point, but more good news. This isn't new. In fact, this conversation was just as rampant in the early Church as it is for us now. And Paul—the great pastor and church planter—understood this conversation. Better yet, he engaged this conversation. He didn't avoid it. He confronted it in the lives of believers with incredible wisdom and grace. In nearly all of his letters you can find some version of this conversation. And it was especially pressing for our friends in the Corinthian church.

12 "I HAVE THE RIGHT TO DO ANYTHING," YOU SAY—BUT NOT EVERY-
THING IS BENEFICIAL. "I HAVE THE RIGHT TO DO ANYTHING"—BUT I
WILL NOT BE MASTERED BY ANYTHING. 13 YOU SAY, "FOOD FOR THE
STOMACH AND THE STOMACH FOR FOOD, AND GOD WILL DESTROY
THEM BOTH." THE BODY, HOWEVER, IS NOT MEANT FOR SEXUAL IM-
MORALITY BUT FOR THE LORD, AND THE LORD FOR THE BODY. 14 BY HIS
POWER GOD RAISED THE LORD FROM THE DEAD, AND HE WILL RAISE US
ALSO. 15 DO YOU NOT KNOW THAT YOUR BODIES ARE MEMBERS OF
CHRIST HIMSELF? SHALL I THEN TAKE THE MEMBERS OF CHRIST AND
UNITE THEM WITH A PROSTITUTE? NEVER! 16 DO YOU NOT KNOW THAT
HE WHO UNITES HIMSELF WITH A PROSTITUTE IS ONE WITH HER IN
BODY? FOR IT IS SAID, "THE TWO WILL BECOME ONE FLESH." 17 BUT
WHOEVER IS UNITED WITH THE LORD IS ONE WITH HIM IN SPIRIT. 18
FLEE FROM SEXUAL IMMORALITY. ALL OTHER SINS A PERSON COMMITS
ARE OUTSIDE THE BODY, BUT WHOEVER SINS SEXUALLY, SINS AGAINST
THEIR OWN BODY. 19 DO YOU NOT KNOW THAT YOUR BODIES ARE TEM-
PLES OF THE HOLY SPIRIT, WHO IS IN YOU, WHOM YOU HAVE RECEIVED
FROM GOD? YOU ARE NOT YOUR OWN; 20 YOU WERE BOUGHT AT A
PRICE. THEREFORE HONOR GOD WITH YOUR BODIES.

(1 COR. 6:12-20)

This is a strange passage, right? At first you have Paul being all
"yes, yes"—"I have the right to do anything." But then he taps the
brakes and appears to be "no-no" when it comes to food and stomachs and bodies. To say the least, I think it's easy to read this passage
and think, "This guy Paul was wonky."

Here's the deal. Corinth was a city that had hundreds and maybe
thousands of shrines to false gods. At many of these shrines there
were "temple prostitutes" who could be purchased for entertain-
ment and pleasure as the practice of worship to their respective gods.
Paul confronts this with "I have a right to do anything," but then

quickly follows with, "but not everything is beneficial." Then he brings up two topics that are going to decisively pull this conversation together. Food and sex. But why these two topics? Why take such differing topics and pull them together? This is the fascinating part of Paul's brilliance. I believe these two topics deeply revealed the appetites and the cravings of not only the Corinthian church but of all humanity. It's not uncommon to consider both of these appetites as deeply connected.

Let's Talk About Sex

Imagine we're standing in a room, and we have two more tables—different than the ones we've been discussing—in front of us. One table (bear with me, this gets weird) is the sex table (I know.) It has candles, chocolates, roses, all the fixings for a nice, romantic evening. The other table, it's just the food table. You could put a pizza box on it. Or maybe a bag of Taco Bell (if you read the last chapter, you get that one.). Each of these tables represent these portions of our lives.

Let's Talk About Food (Again, Briefly)

But, let's pause on the sex and talk about food.

1 NOW ABOUT FOOD SACRIFICED TO IDOLS: WE KNOW THAT "WE ALL POSSESS KNOWLEDGE." BUT KNOWLEDGE PUFFS UP WHILE LOVE BUILDS UP. 2 THOSE WHO THINK THEY KNOW SOMETHING DO NOT YET KNOW AS THEY OUGHT TO KNOW. 3 BUT WHOEVER LOVES GOD IS KNOWN BY GOD.

(1 CORINTHIANS 8:1-3)

Paul spends a chapter and a half (1 Corinthians 6-7) talking about sex and marriage, singleness and faithfulness. And then he makes this transition to food. But not just food, but food sacrificed to idols. And notice this. For Paul, something is different about food. He doesn't lump these things together to say, "Don't have sex and don't eat food that's meant for false idols." Because apparently these believers were eating food at the temples (they were the equivalent of restaurants as we discussed in the previous chapter) and having sex with the prostitutes. It was their Friday night. And Paul deals with the sex very clearly, and then he turns to the food and something is different in his writing.

In these first couple verses, he says this isn't just about knowledge. He says to the folks at Corinth, "I can't answer your question about the rules for food with just information transfer." This is too complex. And it has to be rooted—when it comes to food—*in love*. Paul indicates this isn't black or white— it is going to be gray. There's a lot of room in this discussion for interpretation. And it has to all be colored by love.

Black and White and Gray, Oh My!

When it comes to sex, or intimacy, there are clear standards God has set up to maximize our freedom. Very simple, very clear, biblical standards about sexual purity, the sinfulness of idolatry, Jesus alone as the path to salvation, and all the ways of being in the world that, if we reject them, will cause more harm to our most intimate relationships. It's not to say there aren't layers of complexity behind these conversations; there are. I'm not making light of that. But, ultimately we are invited to freedom *from* sin that gives us freedom *for* the good. Let me say that again: We are invited away *from* sin in order to find freedom *for* good. It may not always be easy, but it's black and white clear.

But when it comes to food, well, we've stumbled into Christian freedom and space for our own understandings of liberty, grace, conscience, and especially love for others. This is where things can get a little gray, and that's okay. Should you watch R-rated movies? What about alcohol? What about secular music? Drums in church? Different translations of the Bible? Whether cats are part of the curse of sin? (I'm kidding, sort of.) Here there is a ton of room and things change based on your own conscience. But above all else, don't forget that these things (drinking, cussing, chewing, or dating girls who do) don't push you closer to God and they don't pull you away from Him. However, you must always keep love for your weaker brothers and sisters in mind. Freedom is about engaging the world in your way being led by God's Spirit.

Freedom?

Freedom is an incredibly difficult word, isn't it? We all want freedom and we all celebrate freedom and we all claim freedom as the basis of our nation, but we all often mean different things with the word. It's kind of like beauty or justice. We love the idea, but we're not all sure we agree on the meaning. Think about it this way. Are you free to drive the wrong way on one-way streets? Of course you are. You are free and hold every ability to do that. But if you do, it will mess with someone else's freedoms, and eventually your own. In the same way, as one great writer said, the freedom of your fist stops where the freedom of my nose begins.

"BE CAREFUL, HOWEVER, THAT THE EXERCISE OF YOUR RIGHTS (FREEDOM) DOES NOT BECOME A STUMBLING BLOCK TO THE WEAK."

(1 COR. 8:9)

Paul suggests that if you are practicing your freedom and it destroys someone else's faith because you didn't have them in mind, you've blown your freedom. He tells the Corinthians, "As a Christ-follower, your freedom always has effects on the people around you." And he takes this love, this freedom wrapped up in love for our brothers and sisters, to an incredible commitment by saying if he himself were to cause someone else to spiritually stumble, he'll give up all the food he can just to guard their hearts.

Paul's Use of Freedom

In the next chapter, Paul carries this conversation to an entirely different level by sharing his passion of how his freedom might be used.

19 THOUGH I AM FREE AND BELONG TO NO ONE, I HAVE MADE MYSELF A SLAVE TO EVERYONE, TO WIN AS MANY AS POSSIBLE. 20 TO THE JEWS I BECAME LIKE A JEW, TO WIN THE JEWS. TO THOSE UNDER THE LAW I BECAME LIKE ONE UNDER THE LAW (THOUGH I MYSELF AM NOT UNDER THE LAW), SO AS TO WIN THOSE UNDER THE LAW. 21 TO THOSE NOT HAVING THE LAW I BECAME LIKE ONE NOT HAVING THE LAW (THOUGH I AM NOT FREE FROM GOD'S LAW BUT AM UNDER CHRIST'S LAW), SO AS TO WIN THOSE NOT HAVING THE LAW. 22 TO THE WEAK I BECAME WEAK, TO WIN THE WEAK. I HAVE BECOME ALL THINGS TO ALL PEOPLE SO THAT BY ALL POSSIBLE MEANS I MIGHT SAVE SOME. 23 I DO ALL THIS FOR THE SAKE OF THE GOSPEL,

THAT I MAY SHARE IN ITS BLESSINGS.

(1 COR. 9:19-23)

I love this Scripture because it shows us so much about the incredible transformation that has taken place in Paul since he met Jesus. He was the one who lived by the rules. He knew what was black and what was white, and he had very little use for anything gray. . He was a Pharisee - a leading religious leader who prided himself on knowing the rules. He was also the one who persecuted and killed Christians because they were outside of his acceptable system. They were too worldly. But when Jesus got ahold of him, check out the transformation.

Forget the rules. Paul lives with a mantra to do whatever it takes to reach any person who doesn't know Christ. For the Jews, he'll avoid the idol food. He will follow the rules of worship. Honor the codes. And for those who are pagans, Paul says I'll dine out every night with them at the temples. I'll go where they are for the sake of Jesus. We gain something about freedom in our Wonky Churches here that I don't want you to miss:

WONKY CHURCH SURVIVAL TIP #11:
ALWAYS USE YOUR FREEDOM TO SET OTHERS FREE.

When Paul discusses his freedom in Christ, he makes it something more than his own right to do what he pleases. He develops his understanding of freedom – and the way we eat our food – as an act of missionary work for the hearts of others. Put simply, the church is called to be everything for everyone.

Haven't we lost sight of this? Haven't we equated the freedom in Christ to the freedom for us? Don't we walk around, whether we're at the table of hedonism (the Electric Slide table) or the table of asceticism (the dumbbell table), acting as if we're the center of the universe? And this is where we've created the Wonkiness of legalism. We've either damaged our witness by practicing freedom in sinful ways that we were never given, or set up rules that were never meant to be rules. The reality is some of us need to tighten up our standards while some of us need to ease up and chill out a little, maybe even a lot. Paul concludes this section of his letter by returning to that opening statement he made:

23 "I HAVE THE RIGHT TO DO ANYTHING," YOU SAY—BUT NOT EVERYTHING IS BENEFICIAL. "I HAVE THE RIGHT TO DO ANYTHING"—BUT NOT EVERYTHING IS CONSTRUCTIVE. 24 NO ONE SHOULD SEEK THEIR OWN GOOD, BUT THE GOOD OF OTHERS. 25 EAT ANYTHING SOLD IN THE MEAT MARKET WITHOUT RAISING QUESTIONS OF CONSCIENCE, 26 FOR, "THE EARTH IS THE LORD'S, AND EVERYTHING IN IT." 27 IF AN UNBELIEVER INVITES YOU TO A MEAL AND YOU WANT TO GO, EAT WHATEVER IS PUT BEFORE YOU WITHOUT RAISING QUESTIONS OF CONSCIENCE. 28 BUT IF SOMEONE SAYS TO YOU, "THIS HAS BEEN OFFERED IN SACRIFICE," THEN DO NOT EAT IT, BOTH FOR THE SAKE OF THE ONE WHO TOLD YOU AND FOR THE SAKE OF CONSCIENCE. 29 I AM REFERRING TO THE OTHER PERSON'S CONSCIENCE, NOT YOURS. FOR WHY IS MY FREEDOM BEING JUDGED BY ANOTHER'S CONSCIENCE? 30 IF I TAKE PART IN THE MEAL WITH THANKFULNESS, WHY AM I DENOUNCED BECAUSE OF SOMETHING I THANK GOD FOR? 31 SO WHETHER YOU EAT OR DRINK OR WHATEVER YOU DO, DO IT ALL FOR THE GLORY OF GOD. 32 DO NOT CAUSE ANYONE TO STUMBLE, WHETHER JEWS, GREEKS OR THE

CHURCH OF GOD—33 EVEN AS I TRY TO PLEASE EVERYONE IN EVERY
WAY. FOR I AM NOT SEEKING MY OWN GOOD
BUT THE GOOD OF MANY, SO THAT THEY MAY BE SAVED.
(1 COR. 10:23-33)

I love this so much. The problem for Paul is not sex. That's clear. Keep it in the context of marriage as God designed it. Honor your spouse and remain celibate in singleness. Again, not always easy, but black and white clear. The best way to practice freedom and love here is to follow God's design.

The gray though? Well, there's all kinds of freedom and choice there. The bigger question at food or reggae music or tattoos is: How are you using your freedom? How are you practicing grace and how are you extending grace? How are you loving others well with your freedom? What does it mean to carry freedom as a missionary work?

Response-Able

So, these two tables. One is the sex (intimacy) table and one is the food table. And they each have their own challenges, don't they? I don't know if you noticed or not, but these tables are also deeply connected. You see, while one table has clear standards and a good design and the other table feels like it's wide open and gray and up to each believer to discern in their own lives, these tables are also deeply connected. They're tied together, even though at times they feel like they're canyons apart.

Whether we're talking about sex or nose rings, there is a deep connection in all this—and it's the connection of *responsibility*. This is where the Church finds itself. Many of you have been hurt by the wonky church because the church didn't handle our responsibility to you well. We were response-averse instead of response-able. Or actually, selfish instead of loving.

Maybe the church dishonored freedom. Maybe it put too many rules on things that were never meant to have rules. Maybe the things that the church defined as too worldly were actually to be enjoyed, given as gifts for you. And yes, you need to honor the weaker brothers and sisters, but for the judgmental Christians who hurt you, they weren't weak, they were just wrong. And they dishonored you.

Or maybe you've seen wonky churches dishonor the designs God created. Whether it was soft teaching that led you to broken sexuality, or false teaching that kept you from understanding Christ alone as your Savior, or whatever it was, the church didn't take responsibility for the truth the Scriptures point out.

We started out talking about two tables. And we've covered a lot of ground since then, but let me close by drawing your attention to a third table.

The third table is the table that every one of us who identifies as a Christ follower has dined at. It's the table of grace. It's the table where a Good Savior waits and invites his sons and daughters to remember that ultimately, the freedom and the design were all meant to lead them to intimacy with Jesus Christ. When the church walks in freedom with responsibility—becoming all things to all people—and when the church maintains integrity by living the design of the relationships God has set up for them, then we begin to set the third table as a Church to invite people to Christ. We become all things to all people, and we set a table where they can meet the Savior—the communion table where all are welcome, and all belong. There's an interesting crowd at that table—some with crew cuts, some with KJVs in their hands, some with tattoos and nose rings, and some, well, you get the picture, right? It's a picture of the Kingdom, a snapshot of the children of God, the response-able people of Grace. And it's a beautiful picture indeed.

Six

Who You Sleep with Matters

A few years ago, I traveled to a pastor's conference that our broader denomination hosted in Detroit. I attend these gatherings not so much for the conference sessions as for the opportunity to hang out with friends and colleagues from across our region. We don't see each other often, and it's always good to have a group of men and women—fellow pastors—to share time with as we vent regarding the wonkiness of each of our respective churches. On this particular trip, we finished a session and decided to go out to eat late that evening. One of the guys with us was from this area and wanted us to see his church's brand-new gathering space. Then, he was excited to take us to a comedy club in his neighborhood. The food was great, he told us, and usually the comedians were excellent. So, off we went.

Now, before I tell you the rest of this story, I should probably invite you into the demographic makeup of my pastor friend group. To do that, let me tell you another story. And just a warning, this one gets a little embarrassing.

Justin, Have You Ever Slept with a Black Man?

Talk about a heading, right?

The year is 2014. I'm in Denver. Our national denominational gathering is taking place over the course of a week and I headed there early to take a class toward my licensure process as a pastor. To save money—because hotel conference centers are ridiculously expensive—I choose my very first AirBNB stay. Because it's just me, I opt for a really cheap version and reserve a space with a sweet couple in an apartment downtown. I'm offered a small bedroom in their tiny, upstairs apartment. When I get there, I find out they own a greyhound dog. An enormous, almost twice the size of their apartment, greyhound dog. A greyhound dog with irritable bowel syndrome.

Seriously.

I wake up one morning after a horrendous night's sleep and the young lady tells me, "You may want to stay out of the bathroom. The dog had explosive diarrhea last night." Um... My introverted spider senses erupt. You only have ONE bathroom. Where am I supposed to go? I'm paying you for this stay (not much, but I am paying). What do you expect? Have you thought of giving your dog to a happy family? In the country? With a lot of space?

So I change clothes and head to the conference at a brisk walk, looking for a public bathroom (wouldn't you?). And all the while wishing I had spent the money on the hotel where the maid changes my sheets as much as I want and there are no four-legged creatures sharing my restroom.

That night, the conference hosts a late night gathering to reconnect with each other and nearly as soon as I walk in the room I'm accosted by three of my best friends in the world— Mack, Matt, and Ja'mel—who proceed to tell me they, too, had reserved a very cheap AirBNB that come to find out is owned by a practicing witch (which they didn't know when they reserved) who photographs people in their underwear (which they didn't know when they reserved) and hangs said photos on the wall throughout her apartment (which didn't show up in the reservation pictures). Apparently, their stay is not going much better than mine. They actually looked amused when I described the explosive greyhound.

I hope you're keeping up.

Later in the evening, Mack calls us from down in the hotel lobby and tells us to come downstairs. Apparently, one of the kinder, less cheap than us, pastors in our conference had heard us sharing our AirBNB nightmares and was now solidifying a room for the four of us at the conference hotel. I couldn't believe it! A hotel room! Continental breakfast! Maids! No smells of marijuana (the couple I stayed with were happy in Denver)! My mind was racing with praise for Jesus over his blessings in this moment. So I emerge from the elevator into the hotel lobby only to be greeted with—

"JUSTIN, HAVE YOU EVER SLEPT WITH A BLACK MAN????"

I should probably mention that my friends Ja'mel and Mack are African American.

And in this moment, blaring across the hotel lobby from the booking table, in front of hundreds of other colleagues in ministry, several hotel employees, and some gray-haired Denver tourists who are now checking their hearing aids, my very extroverted friend Ja'mel decides to seek out my sleep history in the most public way possible.

In case you're wondering, no, I had never slept with a black man. But for the next few days, I did. We shared a glorious hotel bed with no explosive diarrhea greyhound and no practicing witch photographer. Yes, God is indeed good.

The Comedy Club

Now, let's go back to where this chapter began, the night we visited the new church and the comedy club in Detroit. These were the friends I was with on that evening. There were about 8 of us. Five or six were African American and three or so were white. And we were having an incredible evening. The guy's church was amazing. (Pastors get excited over buildings; church planters get *really* excited over buildings). And so, having taken the tour of his new space, we made our way to the comedy club.

Have you ever seen the old Westerns where the cowboy walks up on the old wooden stairs and kicks open the saloon swinging doors only to find the music suddenly stop and every eye in the room staring in his direction because of his arrival? Well, when we entered that comedy club it felt much the same to me as one of three white bodies in the room full of black bodies. There was no music going as we approached, but there was laughter. And when we entered this space, the laughter kind of hit a hiccup. We were seated, eyes on us, and the room kind of went back to its rhythm. At least until the next comedian came on.

He was funny. Very funny. But he kept looking at our table. And after several minutes, he finally walked over to us in the middle of his set, and just simply said:

"I gotta ask, what the hell are all y'all people doing here *together*? What do you *do*?"

Now again, let me give a bit of background. I said this guy was funny. Very funny. What I didn't say was that a great deal of his comedy was laced with profanity and full of vulgar references that could have made anyone blush, let alone a table full of pastors. So, when he asked what we *do*, my friend Ja'mel (the one from the lobby) giddily stammered, "I *gotta* tell him!"

He looked at the comedian as seriously as can be and said, "We're all pastors."

The comedian repeated the word "Pastors" into the microphone, then literally dropped the mic and walked out of the club in horror.

JUSTIN BOWERS, PHD.

After what felt like several minutes, he walked back in to uproarious laughter and picked the mic up and said, "Why didn't y'all tell me you were pastors!? I'm going to hell!"

He continued his set, albeit with less profanity, and the night moved on to the next comedian, who proceeded (like every comedian after him) to build improv routines cracking jokes about the table full of pastors and the diversity we had brought to their evening. I laughed more that night than I had in a long time. And at the same time, I felt pinpointed from those comedians in a way I had never experienced. It was truly a powerful experience.

The interesting thing about that experience though was that earlier in the day my friend Mack sat on a panel at the conference discussing issues of race and how they relate to the Church. He shared a story of his teenage son being thrown to the ground by a police officer while his son's white friends had looked on without any force being shown from the officer toward them. I listened to his story and felt compassion in a very real way. I realized I will never coach my daughters on how to interact with police. I will never coach them about keeping their hands visible, speaking politely, or fearing a routine traffic stop. I realize our lived experiences, as black man and white man, are incredibly different. And then that night, at that comedy club, I walked away from the evening counting it all joy to have laughed, and been laughed at, with my friends and by those comedians in that place.

The Power of Joy

I tell those stories not really to create any lesson here. I tell them because they are stories that have brought joy to my life and made me better through the joy. These stories have impacted me because of the laughter and the richness of friends with different lived experiences than me. Yes, we share stories of the pain of ministry, the loneliness of leadership, and the wonkiness of the Church. We understand much of what we go through, together. But we also have a great deal of differences. My friend Matt and I are both white. But he lives in the city, and I live in rural West Virginia. My friends Mack and Ja'mel are African-American. They, too, live in the city. And their lived experience is incredibly different from mine. But it is also similar. We do ministry in settings where poverty is rampant, drug addiction is rife, and children are at risk. The children of my community are predominately white. The children of their communities are not. And for all of us, the Church is beautiful, and it is wonky.

It feels these days like we are swirling in the conversations surrounding race and diversity, white supremacy and its effects on black lives. It also feels like we have lost our joy. It doesn't take much to find articles, debates, arguments, frustration, and rage regarding these conversations around race. What is much rarer is the power of joy amidst diversity.

For me, those nights with those friends impacted me because of the joy and the laughter. We shared our joy and therefore, our lives. I found myself in their stories, and I believe they found themselves in mine, and it brought us together. What I want to offer you in this chapter is a path the Wonky Church can take to find the fullness of joy in diversity.

From Corinth to Antioch

We've been trekking back and forth a bit in this book. We've moved from Paul's letter to the church at Corinth to the life of the early church in Jerusalem in the book of Acts. What we haven't talked about yet is the emergence of the first church plant—the church at Antioch. So here we go.

Around 300 BC, Seleucid, one of Alexander the Great's generals, founded the city of Antioch. About 300 miles north of Jerusalem, Antioch was the third largest city in Rome with a population of about 500,000 people. Antioch was a global city, built along key trade routes as a gateway to other parts of the Empire, and consisted of a population of both Jews and Gentiles that created an incredibly pluralistic culture. At one point, Cicero complimented the city for its beauty *and* its experiences. The diversity was a gift to all who would enter. It was within this city that the early church at Antioch began to emerge after the persecution of Christians resulted in the death of Stephen—the first Christian martyr (Acts 11:19).

It's important to note something here. Up to the point of Stephen's death, the church and the gospel had stationed itself firmly in Jerusalem. In spite of Jesus' commission to the original disciples to be his witnesses throughout the world, they remained in Jerusalem. Not until Stephen's death would the mission move from Jerusalem to Samaria and Judea, which included Antioch. In fact, Antioch becomes the missional epicenter of the early Church. Two passages speak directly to the makeup of the Antioch church and its impact on the mission of Jesus. Let's look first at Acts 11.

[19] NOW THOSE WHO HAD BEEN SCATTERED BY THE PERSECUTION THAT BROKE OUT WHEN STEPHEN WAS KILLED TRAVELED AS FAR AS PHOENICIA, CYPRUS AND ANTIOCH, SPREADING THE WORD ONLY AMONG JEWS. [20] SOME OF THEM, HOWEVER, MEN FROM CYPRUS AND CYRENE, WENT TO ANTIOCH AND BEGAN TO SPEAK TO GREEKS ALSO, TELLING THEM THE GOOD NEWS ABOUT THE LORD JESUS. [21] THE LORD'S HAND WAS WITH THEM, AND A GREAT NUMBER OF PEOPLE BE-LIEVED AND TURNED TO THE LORD. [22] NEWS OF THIS REACHED THE CHURCH IN JERUSALEM, AND THEY SENT BARNABAS TO ANTIOCH. [23]

*WHEN HE ARRIVED AND SAW WHAT THE GRACE OF GOD HAD DONE, HE
WAS GLAD AND ENCOURAGED THEM ALL TO REMAIN TRUE TO THE
LORD WITH ALL THEIR HEARTS. ²⁴ HE WAS A GOOD MAN, FULL OF THE
HOLY SPIRIT AND FAITH, AND A GREAT NUMBER OF PEOPLE WERE
BROUGHT TO THE LORD. ²⁵ THEN BARNABAS WENT TO TARSUS TO LOOK
FOR SAUL, ²⁶ AND WHEN HE FOUND HIM, HE BROUGHT HIM TO ANTI-
OCH. SO FOR A WHOLE YEAR BARNABAS AND SAUL MET WITH THE
CHURCH AND TAUGHT GREAT NUMBERS OF PEOPLE. THE DISCIPLES
WERE CALLED CHRISTIANS FIRST AT ANTIOCH. ²⁷ DURING THIS TIME
SOME PROPHETS CAME DOWN FROM JERUSALEM TO ANTIOCH. ²⁸ ONE
OF THEM, NAMED AGABUS, STOOD UP AND THROUGH THE SPIRIT PRE-
DICTED THAT A SEVERE FAMINE WOULD SPREAD OVER THE ENTIRE RO-
MAN WORLD. (THIS HAPPENED DURING THE REIGN OF CLAUDIUS.) ²⁹
THE DISCIPLES, AS EACH ONE WAS ABLE, DECIDED TO PROVIDE HELP
FOR THE BROTHERS AND SISTERS LIVING IN JUDEA. ³⁰ THIS THEY DID,
SENDING THEIR GIFT TO THE ELDERS BY BARNABAS AND SAUL.*

(ACTS 11:19-30)

What we see here is a church with incredible potential. For all the wonky stories I've told in this book, the Antioch church doesn't seem so wonky. It is an amazing expression of the Kingdom of God in the midst of the Roman Empire. Notice the Antioch community was born from persecution. The believers who scattered at the death of Stephen were now embodying the community of faith in a new territory. Where the Jerusalem church never seemed to be able to break out of its static territory, Antioch was born on the move. Notice also the joy of celebration at Antioch. Barnabas is their shepherd, and he brings Saul along to celebrate the work of God and continue fueling the flames of discipleship (see chapter 1). Then, and perhaps most fascinating about the church at Antioch, we see the work of God using this tiny church to impact even the "mother ship" church back in Jerusalem. As a prophet foretells a famine to come, it is the Antioch believers who send a generous gift back to Jerusalem to support their continued ministry. Notice where the story of Acts has taken us – away from Jerusalem to the borderlands, on the edge of mission where the Spirit is thriving.

In chapter 13, we see another brief description of the leadership makeup of the Antioch church:

> [1] NOW IN THE CHURCH AT ANTIOCH THERE WERE PROPHETS AND TEACHERS: BARNABAS, SIMEON CALLED NIGER, LUCIUS OF CYRENE, MANAEN (WHO HAD BEEN BROUGHT UP WITH HEROD THE TETRARCH) AND SAUL. [2] WHILE THEY WERE WORSHIPING THE LORD AND FASTING, THE HOLY SPIRIT SAID, "SET APART FOR ME BARNABAS AND SAUL FOR THE WORK TO WHICH I HAVE CALLED THEM." [3] SO AFTER THEY HAD FASTED AND PRAYED, THEY PLACED THEIR HANDS ON THEM AND SENT THEM OFF.
>
> (ACTS 13:1-3)

While these verses briefly list the names of the prophets and teachers at Antioch, much more is being said here than is first noticed. If we look closely at these names, we realize the leadership table at Antioch consisted of a variety of leaders from diverse backgrounds, both culturally and economically. Barnabas was a Levite of the priestly class, and a native of Cyprus (Acts 4:36). Simeon, called Niger, was most likely a Jew (or Jewish convert) of African descent. Lucius is a Gentile (or Jewish with a Roman name) from the North African city of Cyrene. Perhaps most interesting, Manaen had been "brought up with" (literally in the Greek *synthrophos,* or foster brother) of Herod Antipas – the royalty of Galilee. What this means is that Manaen came from the aristocracy, the wealthy upper class of his world. Finally, and perhaps most well-known is Saul, the ex-Pharisee persecutor, the Roman citizen responsible for Stephen's death (and in a roundabout way the birth of the Antioch church). How's that for irony? Each of these individuals now serves the diverse and eclectic church at Antioch.

It can be no accident, then, that the believers at Antioch are the first to be called "Christians." This word—*Christianos*—holds a long record of debate in regard to its significance. Some believe this word was an official government title given to the believers for political or economic reasons. Some see it as a self-designation. And some see it as a mocking and derogatory term given by the broader Antioch community. While the issues around the term are complex, what is clear is that at Antioch the fellowshipping community of Jesus followers displayed a multiplicity of ethnicities and backgrounds in such a way that the broader culture needed a *new name* and *new identity* to even describe the community they were observing.

I know, it's a long path to get here, but I want you to see where this locates us. In this story, Antioch emerges as a kind of second Jerusalem church. What began in Acts with the church at Jerusalem has now expressed itself in Antioch as the *better* Jerusalem church. It seems that the church in Jerusalem lags behind the work of God's Holy Spirit (in theology, practice, and timing), while Antioch emerges on the leading edge of mission – sending money back to Jerusalem, deploying missionaries, experiencing teaching and discipleship, and practicing the multi-ethnic leadership vision of God's kingdom that had always been promised (covenanted) by Yahweh himself. Antioch is not just *an* epicenter of the Jesus movement in the book of Acts; it is now *the* epicenter.

Thank You Jesus

In the summer of 1997, as a seventeen year old high school kid, I had the opportunity to travel to South Africa for three weeks. While there, I journeyed with a short-term mission team sharing the story of Jesus in cities, rural villages, neighborhoods, community homes, and more. One of the most striking memories I have from that trip was the experience of sitting at a table in a juvenile prison. In a country that had recently seen the official end of Apartheid—the system of institutional racial segregation that lasted in South Africa from 1948 until the 1990's—the shocking effects of that system were still felt in every pocket of its society.

Sitting at that table, I watched as a group of teen girls, all inmates in this detention facility, stood and began to sing as our mission team observed. The girls were representative of the country itself: white, black, and Indian. And they sang in languages representative of that same country—Afrikaans, English, and Zulu. They were singing the same simple words over and over again: "Ngiyabonga Jesu... Dankie Jesus... Thank you Jesus..." Even today, more than twenty years later, I have had dreams of that same table and that same song echoing as I sleep. It was one of the most powerful spiritual moments of my life. Full of compassion for these young women—my peers from another country—who had been incarcerated for their mistakes, full of joy because of their joy, and full of hope for the picture of diversity that country might one day embody if the prisoners of systemic racism could overcome their bondage and find a way toward redemption through the grace of Christ.

NGIYBONGA JESU...

DANKIE JESUS...

THANK YOU JESUS...

Surviving the Wonky, Segregated Church

I am writing this chapter as a man who defines myself in many ways. A follower of Jesus. A husband. A daddy. A leader. A pastor. A teacher. A white male from West Virginia. These are pieces of me that constitute my makeup in several different ways. In recent months, and maybe even the past couple years, I've been exploring that last defining mark in more intentional ways than ever before in my life. In a world where conversations, arguments, political posturing, protests, and riots regarding race and equality only seem to be increasing, it seems important that I give some serious consideration to my whiteness.

So I write this section knowing my understanding is limited, as is my experience. But to write a book about surviving the Wonky Church without naming what Dr. King and Billy Graham both said about 11 o'clock on Sunday mornings being the most segregated hour in America would be like visiting Willy Wonka's chocolate factory without taking the ride on the chocolate river boat. It wouldn't make sense. I am limited, but I am learning. I am heartbroken for my brothers and sisters of color, and I am also not the one to speak most clearly of their experiences and their suffering. I am passionate, and nowhere near knowing enough to speak authoritatively. So I offer here some thoughts on surviving the segregated church (with Antioch as our backdrop) without assuming this is the be-all/end-all for how to do this. There are many, many other great(er) resources available that I have listed at the end of this book in the appendix regarding racial righteousness. With all those caveats, here are survival tips as we journey in our wonky, segregated churches.

WONKY CHURCH SURVIVAL TIP #12:
WE MUST LEARN TO NAME THE ILLNESS.

One of the earliest jokes I remember hearing in elementary school had the "N-word" in it. I laughed. I had no idea why it was supposed to be funny—truly I didn't—but I laughed with my friends because they laughed. It was the same experience I had listening to sex jokes in middle school. I didn't get them, but the peer pressure of not being left out of the humor was enough to make me laugh.

In Sunday school as a teenager, I remember the pastor's son playing a game with one of the regular teachers. The kid, a year or so older than me, would come every week this poor guy taught and do the best he could to stump the teacher with some absolutely obscure Bible question. Regardless of the lesson this teacher had planned, this kid would derail any class with his interest in "theology." One particular Sunday, he raised his hand in the middle of the lesson and asked simply, "Where did black people come from?"

The response of the teacher seemed educated; in fact, this particular teacher was one of the smartest people I knew at that age. He proceeded to explain the R-rated version of the Noah story that I had never been taught in church. Turns out, Noah, after leaving the ark and all those smelly animals and annoying family members after 40 days and 40 nights on the water, decided to get drunk and pass out, naked in his tent. His son, Ham, entered the tent and looked at his naked father and then went and told his brothers instead of simply covering Noah up. When Noah wakes up, he curses Ham with these words:

"CURSED BE CANAAN!
THE LOWEST OF SLAVES WILL HE BE TO HIS BROTHERS."
(GEN. 9:25)

I hate even writing these words here, but my Sunday school teacher went on to explain that this is where slavery entered human society and therefore, Ham became, through God's curse, the first "black" person of the darker humanity that would suffer slavery for millennia to come.

Recently, a friend of mine (a white guy in our town) returned home after a day at work and found a flyer on his front porch advertising propaganda from the local chapter of the KKK. My friend is raising his African-American son in our community.

What I didn't realize in that joke in elementary school and in that poor Sunday school teacher's ignorant biblical education is the deep-seated illness facing our society that breaks my heart for my friend and his son. I didn't realize in the joke in elementary school the deep-seated racism my buddy was passing on that had been passed to him from (most likely) the men in his life forwarding that joke along. I didn't realize that my Sunday school teacher was reinterpreting a prevalent line of thinking supporting white supremacy from biblical theology known as the "Curse of Ham" that gave room for slavery to be endorsed.[1]

I didn't recognize these things because I wasn't aware of either the depth or the complexity that racism and white supremacy carried in our society. To some degree, I don't even today. But I'm learning. With my same friends in Denver, after we were out one night to eat, I watched from the backseat of a car as two of my black friends dropped our third black friend off at the street corner and then didn't drive away. I couldn't figure out why. They waited. And waited. And watched our friend slowly cross the street. And I heard them ask each other, "You think he's okay?" And then I saw him turn from the crosswalk and give them a goofy clown wave telling them to go that finally caused them to laugh and drive slowly away. What I would later realize is the nature of Denver as a predominantly white space and the ever-present awareness my African American brothers and sisters carry as they navigate predominantly white spaces every single day.

Surviving the wonky segregated church begins with naming the illness so rampant in our culture right now. We have spent the past twelve years of our political spectrum watching the presidency of the first African American man followed by the presidency of a man who seemingly refuses to denounce white supremacy. In these years, we have seen the racial division in our country enhanced, the anger inflamed, the cries for justice from our brothers and sisters of color growing louder, and the bristling of the white community against the realities of white privilege and white supremacy grow sharper and sharper.

I frankly have no interest in trying to convince you, if you are a white reader, of the illnesses facing us today. As I said earlier, there are enough resources available for you to study and discern the truth of this illness on your own. What I do wish is to simply encourage you to name the illness, to hear the illness, and to *care* about the illness. The painful reality today is these three simple steps seem as difficult for the white church as for any broader pocket of our society. Why can't we name what ails us? Or, why can't we name what ails our brothers and sisters of color?

When my children come to me complaining of a stomach ache, my first response is never, "Well, is your stomach ache even *real*? What did you do to cause this stomachache? Have your choices reflected good or bad decisions that put you in a place where you might get a stomachache? Yes, your stomachache matters, but *all* stomachaches matter." Sounds ridiculous, right!? And yet, today it seems that so many of us as white, wonky Christians want to take this same ridiculous approach rather than doing what any good and loving relative would do when presented with a loved one's stomach ache: "Honey, I'm so sorry you're hurting! How can I help you?" We name the illness. And we empathize with the effects of the illness. And we do what we can to help.

Racism is wrong. White supremacy in any form is evil. Our segregated churches are a plague in the Kingdom of God.

WONKY CHURCH SURVIVAL TIP #13
GO DEEPER THAN HEADLINES.

We won't find simple answers to the issues of racism and religious segregation in two-minute soundbites. Our news media and social media will never do it. Reconciliation will require a depth of interaction that is rare today. We must dig deeper, listen longer, learn as much as we can, and never stop caring. We must befriend and be mentored by those who have different experiences, different relationships, and different cultural contexts than we do. The Kingdom of God has always been more beautiful when the tables are filled like they were at Antioch, andthis should be our goal even today.

Part of naming the illness is naming our own limitations and limited perspectives. When we retain only our preferred news sources or the voices that simply agree with us rather than challenge us, we perpetually fill our minds with headlines that support our already preconceived opinions. As a white male from a rural, Appalachian context, I can't tell you how many times I've been personally challenged, disoriented, uncomfortable, and left wrestling regarding these conversations. In every one of those moments, I am left with a choice: retreat to my preferred context and assumptions (supported by the headlines I believe are credible) or lean into the discomfort of digging deeper and listening, learning, and discovering new ways of thinking. To survive the wonky segregated church, always lean in.

WONKY CHURCH SURVIVAL TIP #14:
DON'T EVER LOSE THE JOY.

Finally, we must never lose the joy of being the community of faith. My friend Ja'mel, yelling in the lobby of that hotel and asking if I'd ever slept with a black man, was capitalizing, in the most humorous way possible, on every insecurity I carried. And to be honest, it wasn't a loving act—he truly is sadistic about embarrassing others. And I love him for it. He drew me and my West Virginian lack of diversity to the center of that moment, and he lightened the mood with humor. What I wonder, even as I've heard his heart and our relationship has deepened, was if the humor was his own defense mechanism for his insecurity as well. Our friendship flourished because of the joy. Besides my family, there are no other human beings in the world that I laugh with as much as I do my brothers that I really met there in Denver for the first time. No one. We love each other because we laugh with each other.

How much angrier can we be today? How afraid can we get? How depressed and anxious must we find ourselves? What if we embodied hope for our segregated churches and our divided world by embodying joy? What if our differences became sources of laughter rather than blame or fear? What if we continued to love each other with smiles and honest transparency about our discomfort and lack of awareness rather than accusing each other through clenched teeth?

Please hear me well. Earlier this year I – like you – watched the video of George Floyd being murdered on the street as a white police officer held his knee on his neck for 8 minutes and 46 seconds. There is nothing to smile about in this, and every other occurrence of white supremacy. Joy doesn't save the day there. Joy doesn't just help us get through these things. I don't see joy as the answer when protest and prophetic leadership are needed. However, I also want to point out that joy is deeper than a smile. Joy is more meaningful and more substantial than laughter. Joy is the soil of love flourishing in the heart. It is not temporary. It is a posture and not a moment. It is something that carries us through pain, even *with* lament, into the hope of God's promises of renewal, restoration, reconciliation, and resurrection. Joy is the source of love that sustains and never fails.

A Couple Tip Toes Forward

I don't know how to move the wonky segregated church to a place of healing. And I don't think I'm the voice that should know. My friends Mack, Ja'mel, Matt, Kevin, Rich, Leeann, Wayne, Darryl, Shaun, and so many others are the ones I'm trying to learn from. They are the voices I thank God for in my life. So this chapter is different than the rest. My survival tips are less prescriptive and more personal. I hope they help. I hope this chapter spins you out and pushes you to read a hundred other books and listen to a hundred other voices of color, indigenous voices, and diverse voices. I hope this chapter sounds less like "the" way forward and more like a couple of tip toe steps that only lead toward a door that you can no longer resist stepping through. I hope.

[1] Lee, Felicia R. "From Noah's Curse to Slavery's Rationale." *New York Times*. 1 Nov. 2003.

Part Two

Strike that. Reverse It.

Let's step back for a minute to Willy Wonka's chocolate factory. The thing that always bothered me about that movie is we don't know what happened to the children. Did Mike Teevee ever make it back to normal, human size? What about Veruca Salt—did she make it out of the trash compactors? Did Violet pop? And Augustus—whatever became of him?

In the first part of this book, I've tried to name and wade our way through the wonky parts of Church world today. We've seen how these are not actually new and unique struggles for our 21st century churches. They're actually issues and sins that have affected the Church, the followers of Jesus, and those who walk away from Jesus, from our earliest infancy as a body of believers in the first century. But I still have some concerns for those of you who have walked away.

Wherever you find yourself in your "walking away," it wouldn't be much of a survival guide if I simply named the issues but didn't address a way forward. In the second part of Wonky, I want to craft some hope. I want to dream with you about what the bride of Christ *can* be. I want to tell you some stories of hope in spite of wonkiness, and I want to invite you to the mission of renewal for the Church.

Pretend this is the sequel to Charlie and the Chocolate Factory, the story of how Veruca, Augustus, Violet, and Mike all found their way back toward belonging in Willy Wonka's crazy little tribe of misfits And the world was better for having them.

Seven

Beyond Sundays

Let's get back to Corinth. In that wonky church, Paul spent a great deal of time offering corrections, criticisms, confrontations, and encouragement. He is – as their shepherd – calling them toward a healthier, thriving version of life as the faith community. He dealt with their unhealthy obsession with leaders, the lack of spiritual maturing, conflict, politics, food and sex, and the nature of the body life expressed in a way that reflects the beauty of Christ's body. And as we round the corner and head for home in this letter, we come across this in chapter 11:

> *"IN THE FOLLOWING DIRECTIVES I HAVE NO PRAISE FOR YOU,*
> *FOR YOUR MEETINGS DO MORE HARM THAN GOOD."*
> *(1 COR. 11:17)*

More harm than good.
More *harm*...
...than *good*.
Your meetings. My meetings. Our Sunday mornings. They cause more harm than good. Ouch.

Paul is mild here compared to what the prophet Amos speaks to the people of Israel a few hundred years earlier. Check this out as the prophet expresses the voice of God:

> *"I HATE, I DESPISE YOUR RELIGIOUS FESTIVALS; YOUR ASSEMBLIES*
> *ARE A STENCH TO ME... AWAY WITH THE NOISE OF YOUR SONGS! I WILL*
> *NOT LISTEN TO THE MUSIC OF YOUR HARPS."*
>
> *(AMOS 5:21, 23)*

Paul goes on in 1 Corinthians 11 to describe the harm caused by these worthless meetings:

> *"IN THE FIRST PLACE, I HEAR THAT WHEN YOU COME TOGETHER AS*
> *A CHURCH, THERE ARE DIVISIONS AMONG YOU... SO THEN, WHEN YOU*
> *COME TOGETHER, IT IS NOT THE LORD'S SUPPER YOU EAT, FOR WHEN*
> *YOU ARE EATING, SOME OF YOU GO AHEAD WITH YOUR OWN PRIVATE*
> *SUPPERS. AS A RESULT, ONE PERSON REMAINS HUNGRY AND ANOTHER*
> *GETS DRUNK."*
>
> *(1 COR. 11:18, 20-21)*

Now a couple of things here. The Corinthian church gathered—like most of the early Church—around a meal. It was called the Lord's Supper, and it was a feast of the best kind. The centerpiece was the bread and wine, the Eucharistic remembrance of the death and shed blood of Christ their Savior. The gathering was the *we* celebrating *He.* There was no stage. No rock bands. No traditional organs. No robed pastors. The meal was the connection point. But, as Paul points out, the meal had grown corrupt. Not only were there divisions (see the previous chapters of this book), the problem was deeper. Divisions were one thing. Mistreatment of the Body of Christ was another. It turns out, individualism reigned in this church as well; for, Paul says, some are starving at the feast and some are consuming so much they're drunk.

What can a pastor and the people do? Paul cuts to the chase: "Let's get back to basics."

The Center of the Feast

> 23 FOR I RECEIVED FROM THE LORD WHAT I ALSO PASSED ON TO YOU: THE LORD JESUS, ON THE NIGHT HE WAS BETRAYED, TOOK BREAD, 24 AND WHEN HE HAD GIVEN THANKS, HE BROKE IT AND SAID, "THIS IS MY BODY, WHICH IS FOR YOU; DO THIS IN REMEMBRANCE OF ME." 25 IN THE SAME WAY, AFTER SUPPER HE TOOK THE CUP, SAYING, "THIS CUP IS THE NEW COVENANT IN MY BLOOD; DO THIS, WHENEVER YOU DRINK IT, IN REMEMBRANCE OF ME." 26 FOR WHENEVER YOU EAT THIS BREAD AND DRINK THIS CUP, YOU PROCLAIM THE LORD'S DEATH UNTIL HE COMES. 27 SO THEN, WHOEVER EATS THE BREAD OR DRINKS THE CUP OF THE LORD IN AN UNWORTHY MANNER WILL BE GUILTY OF SINNING AGAINST THE BODY AND BLOOD OF THE LORD. 28 EVERYONE OUGHT TO EXAMINE THEMSELVES BEFORE THEY EAT OF THE BREAD AND DRINK FROM THE CUP. 29 FOR THOSE WHO EAT AND DRINK WITHOUT DISCERN-ING THE BODY OF CHRIST EAT AND DRINK JUDGMENT ON THEMSELVES.
>
> (1 COR. 11:23-29)

The piece of this passage that has often grown so familiar as the element of our Communion practices is the piece we most often tend to miss. "Everyone ought to examine themselves before they eat of the bread and drink from the cup." Wait, what?! All these divisions. All these arguments. All the wonky crap that defined Corinth (and still defines us), and Paul says "check yourselves?" What about all that other stuff? What about all those other people? What about the problems that are so rampant in the church?

Aren't these the questions we keep asking—both those of us who've been hurt by the church but stayed, and those of us who've been hurt by the church and left? What about all that other stuff? What about those people that hurt *me*? What about the pastor that shamed me with guilt? What about the congregant that couldn't speak without being critical? What about the ones who thought politics had to be central to faith? What about the leaders who couldn't get along? What do we do with all the hurt that keeps us from gathering at the table Jesus invites us to? Paul speaks clearly:

WONKY CHURCH SURVIVAL TIP #15: EXAMINE YOURSELF.

I know. It's not very helpful, is it? It doesn't heal what still hurts us. It doesn't confront the places we were wronged. It seems to let so many others off the hook, doesn't it? Wouldn't you prefer a different approach? I know I would. Don't you wish Paul said something about throwing out the ones who've hurt you so they can't ask for forgiveness? Or it'd have been great if Paul told us to split and form another church across the street from the old church, you know, like a new church plant that fixes all the pain of the old church stump. But Paul doesn't say that, any of that. He simply says, "Examine yourself."

There's a principle here: **When we deal with our own junk, we begin the (incredibly difficult) work of renewing the Wonky Church.** It's true. The ultimate cure for the Wonky Church? Disciples who examine themselves. Disciples who renew their own minds and hearts through the grace and goodness of Jesus rather than waiting for everyone around them to be made right. Paul goes on in this chapter to spell out the simple beauty of how the Eucharist was meant to be taken:

"SO THEN, MY BROTHERS AND SISTERS, WHEN YOU GATHER TO EAT, YOU SHOULD ALL EAT TOGETHER."
(1 COR. 11:33)

Look each other in the eyes. Share the meal face to face. Deal with your own junk, then come to the table. Don't worry about anyone else. Trust that they have the Spirit of Christ at work in them as well and let the table be the same place of grace it has always been, the table that welcomes you in your brokenness with the beauty of forgiveness and the table that welcomes all the other wonky people around you. Go back to the basics. Go back to the center. Let Jesus' forgiveness be for all. Then watch as the church is renewed.

The next chapter of Paul's letter goes on to spell out his theology and understanding of the gifts of the Spirit and their role within the life of the Church. Honestly, to deal in depth with those gifts would require another book, and another discussion of the wonky ways they've been interpreted. So I won't do that here. What I will do, however, is paint a picture using Paul's language—

"JUST AS A BODY, THOUGH ONE, HAS MANY PARTS, BUT ALL ITS MANY PARTS FORM ONE BODY, SO IT IS WITH CHRIST"
(1 COR. 12:12)

—language we use at our faith community here in West Virginia. It is the language of the Church "beyond Sundays." And it has become our own manifesto.

A Manifesto for the Church

New Community exists as, "A people finding and following Jesus *beyond Sundays.*" This language has become our anthem. *Beyond Sundays* entails so much more than a slick logo and catchphrase. It is a theological understanding, a rallying cry for the faith we seek to embody. We want to be ruined from what Church has meant for too long. We want Sundays – as we gather – to be both a celebration and a disruption. We want to celebrate the work of God as a people might tell stories around a campfire. And we want to be disrupted by the sharp edges of God's Word as he continues to call us into the world to enact his Kingdom reign everywhere we go.

We lean into this vision in three ways: Loving God, Loving the Community, and Strengthening Families. Loving God means that at the heart of New Community there is a desire to help people meet Jesus and fall in love with Him. We believe love for God is the fullest essence of what it means to be human. Our Sunday environments are crafted to help people understand God's love and learn to love Him with all their lives. Loving the Community means that as a faith community we exist to help the world flourish. We want to not only love God, but to love the community around us. This means our neighborhoods, our towns, our region, and our world. We are committed to bringing the Kingdom of God to reality by loving our community well. Finally, Strengthening Families recognizes that the world where we find ourselves is watching families dissolve, and part of bringing life to the world means bringing life to our families. One of our greatest passions is helping families grow stronger--no matter what they look like. So, single dads, divorced moms, retired grandparents, and lonely college students are all finding support as they build Christ-centered families.

Years ago, when my wife Carrie and I began to dream about cultivating a faith community from the ground up, we found ourselves identifying with the Jewish exiles the prophet Jeremiah depicts in Jeremiah 29. Sitting by the banks of the river and receiving a letter from God, we heard his words as we heard a call to plant another (wonky) church:

[4] THIS IS WHAT THE LORD ALMIGHTY, THE GOD OF ISRAEL, SAYS TO ALL THOSE I CARRIED INTO EXILE FROM JERUSALEM TO BABYLON: [5] "BUILD HOUSES AND SETTLE DOWN; PLANT GARDENS AND EAT WHAT THEY PRODUCE. [6] MARRY AND HAVE SONS AND DAUGHTERS; FIND WIVES FOR YOUR SONS AND GIVE YOUR DAUGHTERS IN MARRIAGE, SO THAT THEY TOO MAY HAVE SONS AND DAUGHTERS. INCREASE IN NUMBER THERE; DO NOT DECREASE. [7] ALSO, SEEK THE PEACE AND PROSPERITY OF THE CITY TO WHICH I HAVE CARRIED YOU INTO EXILE. PRAY TO THE LORD FOR IT, BECAUSE IF IT PROSPERS, YOU TOO WILL PROSPER." [8] YES, THIS IS WHAT THE LORD ALMIGHTY, THE GOD OF ISRAEL, SAYS: "DO NOT LET THE PROPHETS AND DIVINERS AMONG YOU DECEIVE YOU. DO NOT LISTEN TO THE DREAMS YOU ENCOURAGE THEM TO HAVE. [9] THEY ARE PROPHESYING LIES TO YOU IN MY NAME. I HAVE NOT SENT THEM," DECLARES THE LORD. [10] THIS IS WHAT THE LORD SAYS: "WHEN SEVENTY YEARS ARE COMPLETED FOR BABYLON, I WILL COME TO YOU AND FULFILL MY GOOD PROMISE TO BRING YOU BACK TO THIS PLACE. [11] FOR I KNOW THE PLANS I HAVE FOR YOU," DECLARES THE LORD, "PLANS TO PROSPER YOU AND NOT TO HARM YOU, PLANS TO GIVE YOU HOPE AND A FUTURE. [12] THEN YOU WILL CALL ON ME AND COME AND PRAY TO ME, AND I WILL LISTEN TO YOU. [13] YOU WILL SEEK

ME AND FIND ME WHEN YOU SEEK ME WITH ALL YOUR HEART. [14] I WILL BE FOUND BY YOU," DECLARES THE LORD, "AND WILL BRING YOU BACK FROM CAPTIVITY.[B] I WILL GATHER YOU FROM ALL THE NATIONS AND PLACES WHERE I HAVE BANISHED YOU," DECLARES THE LORD, "AND WILL BRING YOU BACK TO THE PLACE FROM WHICH I CARRIED YOU INTO EXILE."

(JEREMIAH 29:4-14)

As New Community, we find ourselves—as the bride of Christ, his Church!—sitting in exile. If that hasn't been felt in 2020 and 2021, then you are surely too pampered. We find ourselves wondering if we as a church will survive post-pandemic. We find ourselves longing for deliverance and praying for the hurt we've inflicted on so many who have walked away from Jesus at our hands to be healed. We find ourselves clinging to God's call to the exiles. Settle down. Build houses. Plant gardens. Marry. Have sons and daughters and give them in marriage. Seek the peace and prosperity of the cities (or rural towns) where you dwell. Reject the false prophets (of every shape and size). And then, as you live, as you dwell and grow and flourish and make life better for the communities around you because of your trust in Yahweh... as you do those things, trust the plans God has for you because he *will* be found by you.

Our manifesto calls us to love Jesus, cling to Jesus, and trust Jesus in his Lordship over our time and our space. Our manifesto helps us cling to the beautiful, messy, painful work of always holding up the bride of Christ – his Church – as his continued and embodied action in the world around us. Think about that. Jesus came as the extension of God's work – flesh and blood – into the world. He was God in action; and when he left the earth he empowered his apostles to build his body – God's continued action the Church – to keep things rolling. This is the power we are given as his body.

So, perhaps for the last time in this book—*I am sorry*. If we were sharing coffee I'd probably make you uncomfortable with how deeply I feel this statement. I am sorry you've been hurt by the church. I am sorry you've been wounded at the hands of pastors like me. I am sorry the sanctuary of Christ has not felt like a sanctuary. I am, so, truly, sorry. But I am also praying as you read this manifesto that something comes back to life in you. Something like a spark that kindles a fire of hope. Something that whispers – that still, small voice – that pulls you back toward the Heavenly Father and his Son and his Spirit who are and always have been your greatest Lovers. And, I am praying that you find, in that spark, even if it takes years, the hope that the Church—his bride—might one day again be beautiful, and even more beautiful with you sewn into the fabric of its wedding dress.

Like the Israelites living in exile, we at New Community find ourselves in an in-between space. We are, as Jesus followers, living and praying for God's Kingdom to come and his will to be done on earth as in heaven, and we realize that Kingdom invasion began with the life, death, resurrection and ascension of Jesus in his Lordship. Yet we also realize that that invasion is not complete and will only be so when Jesus returns and heaven and earth truly collide in the fullness of what they are meant to be.

As this people of the in-between, we are the Church. We are the Church. We are the Church in all its potential beauty—a place called, as Amos proclaims—to "let justice roll on like a river, righteousness like a never-failing stream!" (Amos 5:24). Our songs may be noisy and dissonant to God at times, but our *beyond Sundays* life, the way we love our community and seek to be the hands and feet of Jesus, that is the stuff of Kingdom dreams.

Our manifesto calls us to acknowledge the grotesque sins of the Church, those of which we are complicit, those we still commit. We have failed to love. We have failed to lament. We have failed to act. We have been found guilty. We're like the children in Willy Wonka's factory—unworthy of the gift of belonging—the grace that still defines the Gospel of Jesus—bestowed upon us. We are the wonky ones. And we have done incredible damage by failing to be the Church that God imagined us to be. And yet, we still believe grace truly is amazing. And so we still believe in the Church. Remember: the Church is a whore, and she is our (beautiful!) mother. So, we press on.

At New Community, we believe in our greater-than values. Relationships are greater than programs. Stories are greater than rules. What we are for is greater than what we are against. We is greater than I. Following Jesus seven days a week is greater than following Jesus one day a week. And speaking of Jesus, well, Jesus is greater than all. Greater than the wonkiness of our fallen leaders. Greater than shallow versions of discipleship that lower the cost of following him. Greater than when well-dressed church folks get really pissed off at each other. Greater than the political idolatry that infects our corporate bodies. Greater than our legalistic pettiness that keeps us from true freedom in Christ. And greater, so much greater than the racism and segregation that divide the beautiful bride of Christ even today. Yes, Jesus is and will always be greater than all.

Eight

Love Jumps in the Pool

I want to start this chapter with a question that gauges your level of parenting. Now I know some of you aren't parents yet. No worries. You get to just stand in superiority over the rest of us and predict how awesome you'll be. Some of you, you were parents, but the little kid days are over. So you get to look back and see how you did. I want you to think about what you would do in this scenario.

It's one of those hot, summer days and you've taken your kids to the pool. Your kids know how to swim. They may be still small, but when they go underwater, they are going to come back up. You get to the pool and your kids are off like bullets. They're in the water. Splashing. Jumping in. Climbing up the ladder. Jumping in again. In this moment, you do what nearly every parent at the pool does. You take your caravan of stuff—the towels, shoes, snacks, and that novel you've been dying to start reading—and you find a good chair where you can watch the kids closely but still find comfort in the sun. Then it happens. It happens every time. Are you ready for it?

In the cutest voice possible, your kids yell up at you with big smiles on their face, "COME SWIM WITH US!!!"

Here's the question: In that moment oh parent, **what do you do?** And here are the options:

Do you—

(A) Jump in immediately. Forget the water temperature. You're cannon-ball-ing your way into the deep end. Let's do this.

(B) Lie/make excuses. "I'll be there in a little bit." (Liar). "I just need to put some more sunscreen on." (Filthy liar). "I'm going to get good and hot first." (Wow, are you still lying!?)

(C) Tell them, "Heck no! You're not going to drown, and I've got a great book to read!"

A, B, or C? I know. It's hard. The thing is as a kid you don't care about anything but swimming in the pool. It could be 50-degree water, but you don't care. You're a kid. But somewhere along the line you stop being a kid and realize that sitting in the sun and reading a book is, well, awesome. That happened to me and I started choosing option (B) above. I started making excuses not to get in the pool. How about you?

Now are you ready for the God part of this?

Love jumps in the pool. In fact, **love *always* jumps in the pool.** Always.

When it comes to our relationship with God, and our relationship with the Church, I think many of us have formed some kind of a relationship with Jesus where he's invited us to swim with him in the pool and we're sitting on the side making excuses, so we don't have to get uncomfortable. In Paul's letter to the Corinthians, he saves his powder keg of writing, his vision for their body of believers, his passion-filled heart cry until the 13th chapter. Then, he unloads. And in that chapter, he casts his own manifesto for the Church (not the wonky Church, the *real* Church) where love is the movement.

I believe we have spent enough time as Christians with our nice, neat little Bible studies and our wholesome Christian romance novels and our little churchy small groups sitting on the sidelines basking in the love of God but not really jumping in the pool of mission with Jesus to engage the movement he has called us to to truly love. When we talk about the renewal of the Church, hope for de-wonkifying the body of Christ, we have to get back to the call to love. We have to reassess, honestly, our lack of love. And we have to determine if we're willing to jump in the pools Jesus invites us to and join the movement Jesus started over two centuries ago – the movement of love.

Two Brave Women and the Man with No Name

In 1854, the famous novel *Uncle Tom's Cabin* was first published by the author Harriett Beecher Stowe. Harriett was an abolitionist and the daughter of a minister. In her book, she told the emotional story of the cruelty of slavery in the U.S. In its first year of print, the novel outsold all sales of the Bible. Printing presses were forced to stay open 24 hours a day to keep up with the public demand. In many ways, Harriett's book was a revolutionary work of fiction.

The story is told that after the Civil War started, Harriett traveled to Washington, D.C., and met President Lincoln. Apparently, Lincoln, a very tall man, looked down at Harriett and said, "So, you are the little woman that wrote the book that started this war?"

In 1955, another young woman, this time an African American woman, sat down in the "coloreds only" section of a bus in Montgomery, Alabama. When the white section filled up and the driver demanded she give up her seat, forty-three year old Rosa Parks refused. Her simple refusal launched a boycott of the Montgomery Bus system that would catalyze much of the Civil Rights movement in the late 50s.

Fast forward to 1989. On June 5, an unidentified protester stepped in front of a column of tanks operated by the Chinese military. Just one day earlier, the military utilized force and killed student protesters who were standing up to China's Communist regime. To this day, no one knows exactly who this protester was. Many stories suggest he was executed just a week or two after his stand in front of the tanks.

Everyone of these individuals understand a simple survival tip for building the movement the Church is called to be:

WONKY CHURCH SURVIVAL TIP #16:
MOVEMENTS ALWAYS COST US SOMETHING.

For Harriett and Rosa, and for this unidentified young man, there were costs to standing up. There were consequences to taking their beliefs and making them public. There was a moment, or a series of moments, where each of them had to take the ideas in their heads and the passions in their hearts and let them see the light of day. And in these moments, love became the movement. Two brave women and the man with no name jumped into the pool, and it cost them a great deal.

The Most Excellent Way

IF I SPEAK IN THE TONGUES OF MEN OR OF ANGELS, BUT DO NOT HAVE LOVE, I AM ONLY A RESOUNDING GONG OR A CLANGING CYMBAL. [2] IF I HAVE THE GIFT OF PROPHECY AND CAN FATHOM ALL MYSTERIES AND ALL KNOWLEDGE, AND IF I HAVE A FAITH THAT CAN MOVE MOUN-TAINS, BUT DO NOT HAVE LOVE, I AM NOTHING. [3] IF I GIVE ALL I POS-SESS TO THE POOR AND GIVE OVER MY BODY TO HARDSHIP THAT I MAY BOAST,[B] BUT DO NOT HAVE LOVE, I GAIN NOTHING. [4] LOVE IS PATIENT, LOVE IS KIND. IT DOES NOT ENVY, IT DOES NOT BOAST, IT IS NOT PROUD. [5] IT DOES NOT DISHONOR OTHERS, IT IS NOT SELF-SEEKING, IT

IS NOT EASILY ANGERED, IT KEEPS NO RECORD OF WRONGS. ⁶ LOVE DOES NOT DELIGHT IN EVIL BUT REJOICES WITH THE TRUTH. ⁷ IT AL-WAYS PROTECTS, ALWAYS TRUSTS, ALWAYS HOPES, ALWAYS PERSE-VERES. ⁸ LOVE NEVER FAILS. BUT WHERE THERE ARE PROPHECIES, THEY WILL CEASE; WHERE THERE ARE TONGUES, THEY WILL BE STILLED; WHERE THERE IS KNOWLEDGE, IT WILL PASS AWAY. ⁹ FOR WE KNOW IN PART AND WE PROPHESY IN PART, ¹⁰ BUT WHEN COMPLETE-NESS COMES, WHAT IS IN PART DISAPPEARS. ¹¹ WHEN I WAS A CHILD, I TALKED LIKE A CHILD, I THOUGHT LIKE A CHILD, I REASONED LIKE A CHILD. WHEN I BECAME A MAN, I PUT THE WAYS OF CHILDHOOD BE-HIND ME. ¹² FOR NOW WE SEE ONLY A REFLECTION AS IN A MIRROR; THEN WE SHALL SEE FACE TO FACE. NOW I KNOW IN PART; THEN I SHALL KNOW FULLY, EVEN AS I AM FULLY KNOWN. ¹³ AND NOW THESE THREE REMAIN: FAITH, HOPE AND LOVE. BUT THE GREATEST OF THESE IS LOVE.

(1 COR. 13:1-13)

Thirteen verses, and two thousand years of power. It's no wonder we still read these words at weddings. They carry commitment and passion, affection and covenant. But it's a wonder we don't read these words more as churches. Paul's "most excellent way" is the way of love— the way of all those who have been a part of movements. It is the way of change, the way of renewal and reimagination. It is the way of Jesus as he picked up the cross and made his way toward Golgotha. The "most excellent way" is the way we come to realize, even today, that the Wonky Church might come to life again.

The Church, at its best, has always been a movement. And movements move. They are not establishments. They are not rooted in centralized buildings and hierarchical leadership full of arrogance and opinions. The best movements are grassroots, and build on idealism and hope, a belief that the future deserves to overcome the present. When the Church has been persecuted in the past, it has thrived. Living against the current of society, loving well in spite of trials, and raising up disciples who know the cost of love have always served as the pulsing heartbeat of the Church that understands the most excellent way.

When Jesus died on the cross, those who believed and followed Him were less than a thousand individuals, by best estimates. No more than 250 years later, the movement of Christianity had spread to cities across Europe and North Africa. Rodney Stark, in his work *The Rise of Christianity*, suggests that from those less than 1,000 believers in 35 AD, the church grew to 40,000 in 150 A.D, 218,000 in 200 A.D., and 1.17 million by 250 A.D.[1] Today, most estimates suggest that there are 2.4 *billion* Jesus followers in the world. As wonky as we are, the Church has not been stopped. The Jesus movement is the most intense movement the world has ever seen. For you who call yourself followers of Jesus over 2,000 years later, you are *still* a part of this same movement of love—the movement that recognizes the pools Jesus invites us to dive into. Yes, I said pool*s*, plural.

Love is the Movement: The Church Pool

I hesitate to write this because I know, for many of you, this is where I'm going to lose you. You made it through the politics section, the sexuality section, and all the other parts you didn't like. But here, I'm going to cause you to check out. To be honest, I wish I could describe a different pool here. But I can't. I believe this to be too true to bypass.

One of the pools we're called to jump (back?) into is the Church. I know. For some of you that sounds like simply too much.

I hope you understand, I get it.

I've wanted to give up and quit on the Church too. Truly, I have. The past year has been hell. From people leaving because of hurt to hurting me because they're leaving, we have seen pain. I've been bad-mouthed. I've fought to not gossip myself. We were forced to move buildings more times than we could count. And every time we did, we lost more folks. Then when all that settled there was this global pandemic that hit, and I realized just how difficult it is to be the Body of Christ. Honest to God, I've been mad enough, sad enough, discouraged enough, frustrated enough a hundred times, that I wanted to go do a different job.

Still, I can't track the line of thinking in Paul as he writes to the Corinthians (or all the other churches he addresses in the New Testament), or the theology of Jesus when he teaches his disciples, or the movement of the early body of believers in Acts without saying to you that I am utterly and entirely convinced that God Himself, the God who crafted the stars and shaped the mountains, has not yet given up on his community of believers called the Church, and neither should we.

The pool of the Church is a mess. I've spent this book describing that to you. Defining it. Processing it. Naming it. Grieving it. Laughing about it. Lamenting it. But it is still the pool God built; and it is, for us as followers of Christ, the water we're called to. I believe we have lost sight of the corporate nature of Church, of what it means to follow Christ. Over forty "one another" statements in the New Testament should let us know just how important our communal life is. Jesus, in his seminal prayer in the Garden of Gethsemane, prays for unity among the body of believers *so that* the world would know God had sent him. Paul builds entire theological constructs from communal metaphors – the *family*, the *living* temple, the *body*, the *ekklesia*. Even in the Old Testament, it is rare to see God speaking without speaking to groups of people. When Adam is created, it is *not good* for him to be alone, and this is before sin ever entered the world. God Himself, even at creation, recognizes the nature of humans needing commonality with others.

I say all this because the hope of this book is not that you simply heal from the wounds the Church has caused you. I do hope for that. I really do. But that isn't the only hope. The other hope, perhaps the larger hope, the thing I long for, is that we would see a movement of Jesus followers reigniting the Church. Not just healing *from* the Church but also working to *heal* the Church. Revival—in the truest sense of the word. Reimagining. Innovation. Creativity that hasn't been experienced in ages. Hope for the bride of Christ to once again live into her calling. But, if we aren't willing to jump back into that pool, how can we ever think the Church will be healed?

Love is the Movement: The Pool of the World

The second pool may be easier to jump in. In fact, you may already be swimming there. It may be natural waters for you. But for those who are still wrapped up in the subculture that often is the Church, this may be more difficult. Remember that sweet mom and her homeschooled daughter I mentioned? Remember how she told me the youth group was the worldliest place where her daughter spent time? Remember how snarky I was to tell her that wasn't a good thing? Well, I wish I could go back and change my response; but my sentiment is still the same. Some of you need to jump out of the Church waters a bit so you can love the world the way Jesus called us to.

For too long, the churchgoers, those of us wrapped up in our piety and busyness with church programs, have disengaged the world around us and failed to embody the hope Jesus promises for the world his Father created. We live in the middle, and those of us who are pastors know this perhaps better than most, of the idolatry of religious programming rather than the mission of relational presence. It's not unheard of to have a worship service on Sunday morning with Bible study on Sunday night, small group on Tuesday, youth group on Wednesday, prayer meeting on Thursday, and several meetings on the off days. With this as a rhythm (or some expression of this rhythm), how can we ever be the salt and light for the cities and towns where we live? Yeah, we can't.

When we read the New Testament, we see in both the life of Jesus and the rhythms of the early Church that a high value for the mission of the Gospel was a presence in the streets. Jesus taught as he traveled. He dined (with sinners and tax collectors!) as a regular occurrence. He found himself with questionable company nearly every, single day. He engaged the public squares. And, when he came to town, life usually got better for those in need. The only people who were commonly upset when Jesus showed up were the religious folks.

The same could be said of the church in Acts. The disciples moved between homes and the temple courts. They spent their time both "praising God and enjoying the favor of all the people".[11] Just consider that statement alone as it compares to our current culture. The writer of Acts says that each day the people who followed Jesus worshipped their Creator *and* had a great reputation with the larger community. Doesn't this sound crazy in our current political, social, relational, and economic settings? The Church either stands fixated on their practice of worship (all the busyness of their programs) or distracted by their community presence (missing the heart of discipleship). Not so in the early Church. They were a part of their world—loving, healing, and serving their communities without compromising their passion for God and his Spirit.

Is this even possible today? I believe so. I believe it is imperative. For the Church to be reimagined, to de-wonkify ourselves, we have to re-engage the world with the same Gospel presence Jesus and his early followers carried. We must be the people that pick up the mantle of Jesus' manifesto as he preached for the very first time:

> "THE SPIRIT OF THE LORD IS ON ME, BECAUSE HE HAS ANOINTED ME TO PROCLAIM GOOD NEWS TO THE POOR. HE HAS SENT ME TO PROCLAIM FREEDOM FOR THE PRISONERS AND RECOVERY OF SIGHT FOR THE BLIND, TO SET THE OPPRESSED FREE, TO PROCLAIM THE YEAR OF THE LORD'S FAVOR."
>
> (LUKE 4:18-19)

But How?

And still, I know what you're thinking. Not all of you. But some of you. The ones who feel like you're still the vagrant. You have no home. The Church was your home, and they hung you out to dry. It hurt too much. It cost too much. And you could never go back.

I do know that pain. I don't know your pain, but I know that pain. And I know the question. As much as you might long to jump back into the pools Jesus invites you to, it just feels like it's too risky. It's not worth the hurt, again. And so, you have that question – *how?* How could I do this again? How could I give the Church, or that pastor, or those people, another chance? It's just too much.

It's the right question. It's the question to which this entire book has led us. It's the question without a simple set of answers, no steps, no clear path. But it's the question that would never be as powerful if there existed simple answers and steps. Instead, this is the question that brings us to the place of beauty, the perspective that can only exist if Jesus is really telling the truth. The *how* of re-engaging the community of Christ's body – the Church – with hope and potential rather than hurt and dread can only be answered by the story, the ultimate story, the only story, of Jesus's life. Not his death, but the life that came through death, the grace that came from the shedding of blood, the great beauty of resurrection.

[1] Stark, Rodney. *The Rise of Christianity: How the Obscure, Marginal Jesus Movement Became the Dominant Religious Force in the Western World in a Few Centuries.* Harper, San Francisco, 1997.

Nine

The Great Glass Elevator

Seeing Through the Smoke

In 2018, I landed at the Sacramento airport on a trip to speak in a friend's church. Just about a hundred miles away from the airport was the Camp Fire raging in Butte County, California. I don't know how much you know about the Camp Fire, but this was the deadliest fire in California's history. The flames caused 85 civilian fatalities and was the most destructive to insured losses in the state's record. It also burned over 153,000 acres of land and destroyed close to 20,000 structures. At one point, the fire's estimated cost of damage was between $7.5 and 10 billion. While I was on this trip, I had dinner with a friend who told me the flames moved at 800 yards per minute and as gusts of wind caught the flames, they would jump up to 500 yards at a time. I remember watching the news as I was there, listening to residents sharing how they had been in the process of fighting the evacuation traffic only to see flames burning on both sides of the freeway around them. Others ran out of gas and had to be picked up by strangers just to make it to safety. It was a terrifying time.

But most fascinating to me in all of this was when my plane descended into Sacramento. Coming down out of the sky things were as clear as you would imagine to be soaring above the clouds. But as we neared the ground there was suddenly a haze that I thought consisted of more clouds. As we pushed on down through this "cloud" it didn't disappear. I realized the entire area was clouded with smoke that was spreading from over 100 miles away.

The effects of this fire, it turned out, had stretched far south to Sacramento and even two hours further to San Francisco. People were being told to wear masks (imagine that!) when they were outside. Schools and colleges shut down. To even walk outside, the smell was overwhelming.

One night, as I walked with my friends to their favorite dinner spot in the city, they turned and asked me, "Do you think the smoke is bad?" My eyes about fell out of my head. I couldn't believe they would ask me that. For the entire week, every time I had been outside I was choking. I was tired of the polluted, smoky air after only 24 hours. And my friend says, "Do you think the smoke is bad?"

Do you know why he asked me that question?

Because for my friend, at that point, the smoke was better than it had been.

For many of us, we're convinced *better* is the new standard for the wonky church. I want to say to you, in the Kingdom of God where resurrection is real, *better* isn't enough. In fact, *better* has never been the goal, not at all. Instead, the goal has always been to create *new*. Not *better*, but *new*.

This is why the Apostle Paul, after so much time confronting the wonky church at Corinth with the issues that were destroying them, reaffirms their hope by pointing their story toward resurrection. Near the end of his letter, Paul isn't interested in simply confronting the church and trying to make them *better*; he's much more passionate at seeing them made *new*. In fact, in his second letter to the Corinthians he makes this abundantly clear:

"THEREFORE, IF ANYONE IS IN CHRIST, THE NEW CREATION HAS
COME.
THE OLD HAS GONE, THE NEW IS HERE!"
(2 COR. 5:17)

I love this. I love the exuberance Paul spouts here. It's like he can't contain the passion in writing to the wonkiest of churches and letting them know that their hope—for any and all ways forward—is not in improvement, self-help, or steps toward growth. Those things are, as Paul says in 1 Cor. 15, futile. Worthless. Hopeless. No, for the wonky church, it is only resurrection that moves them forward, onward, and upward... like a great glass elevator.

The Great Glass Elevator

To end this conversation, we have to return to where we started. Willy Wonka and that great chocolate factory he invited Charlie Bucket to explore. If we could go back to the very introduction of this book, you may remember the wonky moment in that film when Gene Wilder, playing Willy Wonka, unhinges the character with his move from a decrepit and mysterious man on a cane to a nimble tuck and roll that leaves us all wondering just what sort of man this might be? This was where we met Wonka, but it is not at all where we end with him.

If you haven't seen the film, you're missing out. If you have, you know exactly what I'm talking about. The film moves forward with each of the lucky children having their own vices revealed and missing the opportunity to see the rest of the factory. Augustus Gloop is sucked into a tube of chocolate for giving himself to his gluttonous obsessions. Veruca Salt is tossed down a trash bin for being too greedy. Violet Beauregarde blimps out to a blueberry due to her pride. And Mike Teevee is shrunken to nearly nothing because of his great addiction to television, with the desire to become the very thing that consumes him. But, what about Charlie?

The poverty-stricken, innocent child-protagonist of the film moves through the tour and is abruptly told to leave by Wonka because he stole the fizzy-lifting drink. In the unsettling way that Wilder's character plays Wonka, it is a painful moment. It is a moment where Charlie has enjoyed the factory and is now being rejected. However, before he goes, Charlie places his gift back on Wonka's desk. The everlasting gobstopper given to him to take home is the very gift he renders back to its creator. It is a moment of surrender, and if we stretch the metaphor far enough, perhaps also repentance. This is the moment we see Wonka's countenance change. This is the moment where the mystery of the chocolatier is finally unveiled. He really is *good*. There is forgiveness, joy, excitement, and a sudden invitation to Charlie and his grandfather to join Wonka for a ride in the great, glass, elevator. Again, if you haven't, go to Youtube and search for "Willy Wonka and the Chocolate Factory Elevator Scene". Watch the clip.

I always loved this scene because it makes the story finally make sense. All the chaos of the factory, all the oddity of Willy Wonka, all the silly vices of the other characters—it suddenly came together as Wonka floats high above the city with Charlie and his grandfather and offers to Charlie the gift of the factory. "It's yours," he tells him. Everything is well in this moment in the story, finally.

Paul's Great Glass Elevator

In the fifteenth chapter of Paul's letter to the Corinthians, he finally reaches the pinnacle of his theology for the wonky church:

"12 BUT IF IT IS PREACHED THAT CHRIST HAS BEEN RAISED FROM THE DEAD, HOW CAN SOME OF YOU SAY THAT THERE IS NO RESURRECTION OF THE DEAD? 13 IF THERE IS NO RESURRECTION OF THE DEAD, THEN NOT EVEN CHRIST HAS BEEN RAISED. 14 AND IF CHRIST HAS NOT BEEN RAISED, OUR PREACHING IS USELESS AND SO IS YOUR FAITH."
(1 COR. 15:12-14)

In all the wonkiness of this early Christian church, Paul spends this chapter calling them back to the root of their life together. Apparently, this church consisted of folks who believed that the promise of resurrection was simply a façade. Yes, Jesus mattered. Yes, they were following him. But all that life after death stuff? Forget that. That was silly. And Paul can't stand it. It's almost as if he's calling the congregation to lean in close to listen to him whisper these words. After all the silliness, all the wonkiness, after all the ridiculous arguments about which leader was best, what sex and food had to do with freedom, how idols should be treated—after all of that he calls them close and simply whispers this to their hearts: *"...if Christ has not been raised, our preaching is useless, and so is your faith."* Another survival tip:

WONKY CHURCH SURVIVAL TIP #17
LET RESURRECTION PAVE THE WAY FOR RENEWAL;
EVEN RENEWAL OF THE WONKY CHURCH.

This whole Church thing, as wonky as it is? It has *always* been about resurrection. Period. Nothing else. Without resurrection, our faith is still useless, and so is this book.

But. But. I wish I could sit with you and say this out loud, so you hear the passion in my heart coming through my voice. But. If resurrection is real, and I believe it is, then renewal is always possible. The dead don't stay dead. Not dead people. Not dead churches. Not even wonky churches. We, as the people of Jesus, have always been moving toward resurrection, and we can't stop now. We have to ride that elevator of resurrection right through the glass ceiling of the church's wonkiness and learn to see the world (and the Church) in a new way, because God is handing us the Kingdom he's been establishing ever since Jesus came out of the grave victorious over death.

1 in 5???

In many ways, this book has been about seeing the smoke desecrating our churches for what it is—a haze that has polluted and choked the life out of who we were called to be. I want us to see re*new*al, not just *better*ment. My deepest longing here is that the Church—and those of you courageous enough to re-engage or keep engaging the Church—will find new life.

I began writing Wonky a couple years ago. It was born of the same passion you've felt throughout the book. I wanted to offer a portrait of hope for the "Dones," those who had given up on the body of Christ because of the members of the body of Christ. I wanted to name the things that we have avoided for too long. I wanted to repent for my own complicities in the "we" that is the Church.

What I didn't realize when I started Wonky, however, was the way 2020 would ignite the embers of the crisis facing the Church. It has been said that any crisis is an accelerator, and 2020 has proven to be a furnace of acceleration. With the onset of Covid-19 as a global force bringing our systems (including our church gatherings) to a halt, as well as the political rifts that are destroying the U.S. right now, we find ourselves in that accelerator of crisis like the young, first time rider of a roller coaster they never wanted to be on. It has been predicted that 1 in 5 churches will close due to the pandemic.[1] David Kinnaman, the president of the Barna Group, says that "Churches are recognizing... the relationships... they thought were much deeper with people were actually not as deep as they expected".

And yet, resurrection.

Willy Wonka sees the humility of Charlie Bucket and takes him up in the great, glass elevator to hand him the keys to his factory.

Jesus looks at Peter, the very one who would betray him in just a few days time and says he will be the rock of his church, "and the gates of hell will not overcome it" (Matthew 16:19).

And yet, resurrection.

So, here we are at the conclusion, I simply want to call you to keep asking one, simple question.

What If?

What if Jesus was telling the truth? What if hell—in all its schemes and all its spreading of wonkiness—will truly never prevail? What if God isn't finished with the Church, but he truly does want to re*new* it? What if resurrection is more than salvation for eternity but also imagination for the present? What if we, all of us, the ones who keep fighting with the Church and the ones who walked away long ago, what if we are still called to the work that will not be thwarted? I want to offer you one more survival tip:

WONKY CHURCH SURVIVAL TIP #18:
DON'T. EVER. GIVE. UP.

You've wanted to give up. I've wanted to give up. Maybe you have given up. Maybe the Church just hurts too much. And, given where we are culturally right now, with the landscape of pandemic and politics, of race and riots, of hypocrisy and hyper-sensitivity, it would make sense to me.

But I still believe in resurrection, even for the Church.

Maybe this book carries my own repentance for the times I've created the wonkiness. Maybe it's about seeking forgiveness. Maybe it's a vain attempt at trying to make some things right that I know I got wrong or trying to reclaim the beauty of those stars or that calling to ministry on the streets of South Africa. Regardless, it's the best I have. And when all is said and done, these words are offered like that same magical glass elevator shattering through the roof of the wondrous factory and giving a view of the world that all the Charlie Buckets have never imagined. I'm praying, with the hope of resurrection, that you learn to see the Church and the world through the eyes of renewal... and that we all, the brothers and sisters in Christ, the children of God, might never... give... up.

The Church is a whore, and she is our mother.

May we love her well.

If she's hurt you, may you find the love again.

[1] "Research: 1 in 5 Churches May Close Due to Pandemic." *Outreach Magazine website*. 9 Sep. 2020.

ACKNOWLEDGMENTS

This is a book about community. More than the trendy buzz-word that has taken our broader culture by storm, this is about the Christ-community, and all the difficulty that comes with it. This is a book about the wonder that I believe still exists for the beautifully broken Church as Jesus originally imagined it. To write a book like this would have been impossible without my own community around me, and for each of them I am indescribably grateful.

To Matt, Chip, Rich, Mack, Shaun, Darryl, Ja'mel and so many other pastoral colleagues. Thanks for attending conferences just so we could go out to eat and laugh and mourn together as we navigate the call to ministry. You are heroes and friends, and those things rarely co-exist.

To Kevin. I sought a mentor for years. You became more than that. A friend, a brother, a mentor, and an encouragement to use the voice God has given me only as it expresses his love. Thank you for your life.

To the people of New Community. You are the fulfillment of a dream God whispered to me twenty years ago. A dream of what the Church could be. Along our journey I have failed you so many times and only added to the wonkiness, and yet you still embrace me as one of those crazy guides called Pastor. Thank you.

Thanks to Kris Camealy for coaching along the way and encouragement to put in the work. And thanks to John Blase for being the most incredible editor I've ever had (and of course, the only one, but I'm pretty sure I lucked out!).

To my family.

Mom and dad. Everything I've ever written (aside from the boring dissertation) you read and cherished. That alone created the inspiration to believe I could finish this work.

Bec. Thank you for asking how I am regularly, and meaning it.

Malia, Pressley, Isabella, and Stephanie. It is the greatest joy in my life to hear your voices call me daddy. When my insides crumble, that simple word restores. I hope you find in these pages a love poured out on your behalf.

Finally, to Carrie. For twenty years you've journeyed with me, inspired me, dreamed with me, wept with me, cussed with me, and simply continued to embrace the call we have together. I love you so much, and I cannot imagine life without you.

Please note these are merely a *starting point* for digging into these topics with greater clarity and depth. By no means are they comprehensive, and they serve merely as a primer for further conversation.

Further Reading Regarding Sexuality from Biblical Perspectives

- *Redeeming Sex* - Debra Hirsch
- *Talking Back to Purity Culture* - Rachel Joy Welcher
- *Gay Girl, Good God* - Jackie Hill Perry
- *Real Sex* - Lauren Winner

Further Reading Regarding Racial Reconciliation

- *White Awake* - Daniel Hill
- *Rediscipling the White Church* - David Swanson
- *The Color of Compromise* - Jemar Tisby
- *Rethinking Incarceration* - Dominique DuBois Gilliard
- *Trouble I've Seen* - Drew G.I. Hart
- *Jesus and the Disinherited* - Howard Thurman

18 SURVIVAL TIPS FOR FOLLOWING JESUS
WHEN YOU HATE THE CHURCH

Focus on Jesus more than your pastor.

Every leader has a story.

Don't ever follow a leader who's forgotten their own story.

Stop nursing from leaders when you're invited to feast with the King.

Your relationship with Jesus must be stronger than your relationship to the church.

Find a faith community where life in Jesus is consistently proclaimed.

Committing to the church carries with the responsibility to protect the integrity of God's presence among his people.

For unity to exist we must relinquish the right to be right.

Don't ever expect the intersection of the church and politics to be easy.

We have to come clean about our idols.

We cannot be so fixated on freedom for *me* that we forget love for the *we*.

Always use your freedom to set others free.

We must learn to name the illness.

Go deeper than the headlines.

Don't ever lost the joy.Examine yourself.

Movements always cost us something.

Don't. Ever. Give. Up.